100 Things I Wish I Knew in My Baby's First Year

Keys to Making Parenting Easier and Baby Happier

Second Edition

Randy Dean and Lorri Gorno

Paragon House
St. Paul, Minnesota

**649.1
D34O
2011**

First Edition 2004
Second Edition 2011

Published in the United States by
Paragon House
1925 Oakcrest Avenue
St. Paul, MN 55113

Copyright © 2004, 2011 by Randy Dean and Lorri Gorno

Library of Congress Cataloging-in-Publication Data

Dean, Randy, 1965-
  100 things I wish I knew in my baby's first year : keys to making parenting easier and baby happier / Randy Dean and Lorri Gorno. -- 2nd ed.
    p. cm.
  Summary: "Advice for parents covering all major topics of care for babies. It combines advice from parenting experts, research, and hands-on parenting experience. Every topic was extensively researched. The second edition is informed by feedback from researchers, pediatricians, and parents"--Provided by publisher.
    ISBN 978-1-55778-897-9 (pbk. : alk. paper) 1. Parenting. 2. Infants--Care. 3. Infants--Development. I. Gorno, Lorri, 1965- II. Title. III. Title: One hundred things I wish I knew in my baby's first year.
  HQ755.8.D4 2011
  649.1--dc23
                    2011034902

The paper used in this publication meets the minimum requirements of American National Standard for Information Sciences—Permanence of Paper for Printed Library Materials, ANSIZ39.48-1984.

Manufactured in the United States of America
10 9 8 7 6 5 4 3 2 1

For current information about all releases from Paragon House,
visit the web site at: www.ParagonHouse.com

To our children

*For all that they taught us
during that amazing first year*

Contents

Foreword

AS A PEDIATRICIAN with almost ten years of experience and with two children of my own, I find that the best advice for new parents is a blend of evidence-based medicine combined with personal experience. I have read numerous textbooks and journals and I strongly believe that the best education is that gained from actual parenting. While I learned a great deal during my pediatric internship and residency, my deepest and fastest learning occurred from the education I gained practicing pediatrics while working with my wife to raise our children.

After reading *100 Things I Wish I Knew in My Baby's First Year* I was impressed with how closely this book matched what I tell or would like to tell to new parents. As I read, I turned over page corners for each piece of advice that was helpful and applicable. I ceased the page turning since I had turned over most of the page corners. Some of the advice was so perfect that it made me say, "great advice" out loud. If I wrote a book about realistically preparing for and taking care of a newborn, it would closely resemble *100 Things I Wish I Knew in My Baby's First Year's* approach.

There are many books that are focused on taking care of an infant. Some are based on hard evidence and some are based on anecdotal experience. This book is a combination of both, relying not only on advice from parenting experts and research but also on hands-on parenting experience. There is a balance to be found between the teachings found in a textbook and the education gained from personal involvement. *100 Things I Wish I Knew in My Baby's First Year* has found that balance.

This book will answer many questions that expecting parents and the parents of newborns typically have. Common sense and realistic attitudes are an important part of raising healthy and happy children. In pediatrics, there is so much advice offered by so many people, and it is important to find the appropriate answers for common parental concerns. Nothing replaces common sense and personal experience when it comes to parenting and the difficult part is conveying that information. *100 Things I Wish I Knew in My Baby's First Year* has done an excellent job of conveying some of the most important lessons for new parents in an easy-to-read and enjoyable manner.

—David Geller, M.D.
Clinical Instructor in Pediactrics, Harvard Medical School

Introduction

00 Things I Wish I Knew in My Baby's First Year is the result of a crash course in parenting. We were blessed with the birth of three children within one year. Our son was born in April of 2001 and our son and daughter twins came along prematurely in the fall of the same year. This sudden gift of three babies forced us to learn very quickly. Changing thirty diapers a day and the many other tasks needed to raise three infants helped us to perfect our skills and find ways to make parenting tasks easier. When our fourth child arrived in 2006, we again got to take that marvelous journey through a baby's first year and learn even more. As we write this second edition, we are celebrating the recent birth of our fifth child and looking forward to another amazing first year.

The recommendations that we offer in this book started with observations of what did and did not work with our babies. We received excellent advice from some great parents, and we pass this wisdom on in several of our topics. Because we are giving advice on a subject that is incredibly important, our observations alone were not enough. In addition to relying on our real life experience, every topic was extensively researched and each section of this book was reviewed by prominent researchers, pediatricians, and infant specialists. For instance, the section on the safety of vaccines was reviewed by the Director of the Center for Disease Control in Atlanta.

100 Things I Wish I Knew in My Baby's First Year covers a wide variety of information about parenting. Several of the items address infant sleep issues. Getting your baby to sleep through the night and develop good sleep habits is one of the most important goals in your baby's first year. A family cannot function at its best if a baby is having sleep problems. After discussing sleep problems with a great many parents, we found that infant sleep problems are the number one concern for most parents. Fortunately, sleep problems can be avoided by following some simple guidelines. Even if you are picking this book up when your baby is six months old, our suggestions can help you get your baby's sleep problems back under control.

This book is organized chronologically. The book begins with topics that relate to birth and newborns and ends with items that are important as your baby reaches nine to twelve months of age. Each topic is designed to stand alone and has been kept as short as possible to help a busy new parent. There are five appendices at the end of the book that we think you will find helpful. Whether you are reading this book while you are expecting, just after delivery, or months after your baby's birth, we believe you will find information here that will make parenting easier and your baby happier.

Happy Parenting!

There Are No "Perfect" Parents

Everyone wants to be the best parent they can be. It is easy to question your parenting skills on days when your baby is being particularly fussy or difficult. Also of concern can be the tales you may hear from other parents of the many things they are doing to help their child's development, such as using flash cards and going to special classes. There is no one correct way to raise a baby. Although this book offers the lessons that we have learned while raising our children, we strongly recommend that you trust your instincts when making parenting decisions.

As long as your baby is properly fed, cared for, and loved, you are providing for his critical needs. By spending time with your baby and being responsive to his needs, you are being a good parent. Only you can decide exactly how to nurture and support your child's development.

Our advice is to routinely examine how your baby is doing. If you think that there is a problem, then discuss it with your partner and pediatrician. Being a good parent is an ongoing learning experience. You won't always get it right, but no parent does. Fortunately, doing your best as a parent is usually good enough.

Schedule, Schedule, Schedule

When asked for advice by new parents, our first tip is to implement a consistent schedule. Scheduling was a key to a successful first year for our family. Arranging your baby's day around a flexible schedule offers many benefits. A schedule helps your baby regulate her digestive system, sleep through the night earlier, and learn to soothe herself. Scheduling makes parenting easier because you will know what to expect from your baby during the day. This eliminates much of the guesswork about why your baby may be fussing or crying. In addition, a schedule provides a sense of security for your baby because she can count on consistent meal times and bed times.

The first step to getting your baby on a schedule is to feed her at consistent intervals during the day. Start your baby on a set 2½ hour schedule after she is a week old. A 2½ hour feeding schedule means that a maximum of 2½ hours should elapse between the start of one feeding and the start of the next feeding. If your baby is hungry sooner than 2½ hours, then go ahead and feed her. Nurse or bottle feed her every 2½ hours in the following sequence: feed, awake time, then sleep time. In the beginning, you may need to awaken your baby during the day for some of the feedings. Even though it may seem counter-intuitive to wake a sleeping baby, do it!

At night, feed your baby right before bed and then let her sleep until she awakens. If your baby is tolerating this schedule well, you can experiment with a 3 hour schedule. However, we recommend that you stay on a 2½ to 3 hour daytime schedule until your baby is sleeping at least seven hours at night. A few weeks after your little one has mastered sleeping through the night, you can increase your schedule to 3 ½ hour feeding intervals. As your baby gets older, the schedule will lengthen until at one year of age your baby should be eating three meals a day with a bottle or snack before bed.

Some caregivers feel that scheduling is too hard or that it may be difficult on a baby. Our experience, and that of countless others, is that instituting a consistent but flexible schedule helps to make parenting easier and baby happier.

At one time, it was common for pediatricians to recommend a 4 hour feeding schedule for newborns. While some babies did fine on this type of a schedule, most babies need to eat much more frequently in their first months of life. The goal is to introduce consistency in your baby's schedule, but you need to feed him when he is hungry. We found with our five children (four of whom were premature) that within less than a week after instituting a schedule they would start to show signs of hunger almost exactly every 2½ hours. You could almost set your watch by when they got hungry! However, if your baby is premature or underweight, then please be sure to follow your pediatrician's recommendations regarding feeding frequency.

One study of babies fed on demand compared to babies fed using a schedule showed some interesting results. After one month, both groups of babies gained the same amount of weight. However, there was one important difference. The babies that were fed on a schedule required fewer daily feedings (six to eight times per day) compared to the babies that were fed on demand who required feedings nine to twelve times a day.

Getting a baby on a schedule requires effort and consistency. However, this effort will be amply rewarded by making your parenting job easier and your baby happier. We include sample schedules at the back of this book.

When to Take Baby Out in Public

I n general, it is safe to take your baby out as early as his first week of life. Most babies will need to venture out during the first two weeks for their first doctor's appointment. Heading out to other locations is generally fine too. The concern that some doctors have is that exposure to other people and places may increase the risk of infection (although it seems more likely to us that your baby will be exposed to a virus at a doctor's office compared to a coffee shop or grocery store).

Just being out isn't likely to cause an illness. A virus or infection is more likely to come from people who may be touching your baby, particularly her hands, or if you are in a confined area where someone is coughing or sneezing. It is a good idea to avoid people who are sick when you are out and to not allow anyone who hasn't washed their hands thoroughly to touch your baby. It is especially important to ask people not to touch your baby's hands since she is likely to put her fingers and thumbs in her mouth.

If your baby is premature or has a chronic lung condition you may want to be extra careful and limit her exposure to other people during her first couple of months. One virus that can be dangerous for premature babies is RSV (respiratory synctial virus). RSV is the #1 cause of hospitalization for infants younger than one year. Here are some steps to help reduce the risk of exposure of RSV for your baby:

- Try to avoid crowded areas (like Chuck E Cheese at lunchtime on a Saturday!) Keep anyone who is sick or has a cold away from your baby.

- Don't smoke or allow others to smoke around the baby.

- Always wash your hands thoroughly and ensure that anyone else who will be holding your baby has washed their hands.

By following some simple precautions you and your baby can be out and about as soon as you are both ready.

How to Pick the Perfect Pediatrician

When we learned that we were going to be parents, one of our first tasks was to find a pediatrician. Most books we read recommended interviewing several doctors before choosing one. While the recommendation sounded like a great idea, the reality was that neither we nor most of the pediatricians we talked to had the time to spend in a lengthy interview.

We found our pediatrician through recommendations from several trusted friends and acquaintances with children. Be attentive to pediatricians who receive multiple recommendations. We also asked our friends why they recommended their pediatrician. This information allowed us to see if the pediatrician's style and theory were compatible with what we wanted for our child.

The pediatrician's staff is also very important. We ruled out several pediatricians because our friends said the doctor was great, but that the staff and nurses were difficult. We chose our doctor over others because of the high quality of his staff and the easy availability of a nurse to help answer our questions.

Some pediatricians' offices have nurses available during normal business hours to answer questions. We found it very reassuring to be able to get an expert's opinion when we weren't sure if our baby was sick enough to warrant a doctor's appointment. We strongly recommend you find a practice that gives you a doctor you like and trust and a staff that is available to answer questions.

Breast Is Best

The experts agree—breastfeeding is the best way to feed your baby. Breastfeeding provides your baby with the most perfect form of nutrition and gives important skin-to-skin contact.

If you are pregnant while you are reading this book and you plan to breastfeed, you can take some important steps now to prepare. First, attend a class on breastfeeding. Many hospitals offer breastfeeding classes as part of birth preparation. These classes are a great introduction to nursing and we highly recommend that both parents attend. Two sets of eyes and ears are always better than one. Talk with other women you know who have breastfed, read books and visit websites to accumulate a wealth of information and support before your baby arrives. During your last trimester of your pregnancy, get fitted for a nursing bra. Check with your hospital or obstetrician for stores that specialize in nursing apparel and equipment. I was scheduled for my fitting on the day I delivered our twins, so learn from me and don't wait too long.

Before the big day, make sure that your obstetrician and the hospital know that you are planning to breastfeed. This will insure that the staff will not feed your baby, but will instead present her to you for the first feeding. When put to the breast, some babies know just what to do, while others need some help. Do not be discouraged! Remember, both you and your baby are learning a new skill. During the first few days after your baby is born, you will produce colostrum. Colostrum is high in carbohydrates, antibodies and protein, which goes a long way to growing a healthy baby. Unlike some infant formulas, colostrum is easy to digest for your new baby. As if that wasn't enough, colostrum acts as a laxative, aiding your baby to pass her first stools. Your milk should start to come in on the third or fourth day after your baby's birth. At this point, your milk will increase in volume and will be thinner and lighter in color than the colostrum.

Because your breasts don't come with little ounce markers like bottles, many new mothers worry that their baby may not be getting enough to eat. The experts offer these important indicators that your baby is getting enough milk:

1. Your baby nurses at least 8-12 times in a 24 hour period.

2. Your baby is gaining weight (usually between 4 and 7 ounces per week).

3. She is having at least 5-6 wet diapers per day.

4. You baby is alert, active and has good color.

Make sure that both you and your pediatrician are using growth and height charts specifically for babies that are breastfed. Breastfed babies tend to gain weight at a slower rate than bottle fed babies and this difference is reflected in the breastfed baby growth chart. If you have any reservations or concerns about whether your baby is getting enough to eat, talk to your pediatrician.

If you have a cesarean delivery, you can still breastfeed following delivery. Due to anesthesia and tenderness in your abdomen, you may need some assistance holding your baby right away. Don't let this stop you. Ask your husband or a nurse for some help holding the baby and getting her to latch on to your breast. Most of the painkillers and medications used during and after a cesarean section are not harmful to baby, but may make baby a little sleepier at first. The traditional cradle hold may be difficult because of your incision site. Instead, try a football hold (where the baby's body lies beside you instead of on you).

Breastfeeding is a wonderful thing for both you and your baby and we strongly encourage you to try it. However, if you choose not to breastfeed or cannot breastfeed for medical reasons, be confident in your decision and see our tips on formula feeding later in the book.

Swaddle Your Baby for Better Sleep

Swaddling can be an amazing help in your baby's first two months of life. Our experience was that our babies slept much better when they were swaddled. When our fourth child was born, she had some difficulty sleeping at first. We remembered the effectiveness of swaddling and noticed a big change in her sleep habits when she was swaddled.

There are several advantages to swaddling your infant in her first weeks of life. A recent review of past swaddling studies published in the July 2007 edition of Pediatrics described the benefits of swaddling as follows: "We have systematically reviewed all articles on swaddling to evaluate its possible benefits and disadvantages. In general, swaddled infants arouse less and sleep longer. Preterm infants have shown improved neuromuscular development, less physiologic distress, better motor organization, and more self-regulatory ability when they are swaddled. When compared with massage, excessively crying infants cried less when swaddled, and swaddling can soothe pain in infants. It can be helpful in regulating temperature but can also cause hyperthermia when misapplied." There are three important things to keep in mind when swaddling your baby: (1) use a lightweight blanket to keep baby from over heating, (2) to prevent hip problems, don't swaddle too tight around the baby's hip area, and (3) a swaddled baby must still be placed on her back to sleep to prevent the risk of SIDS.

Most importantly from our standpoint was that our babies slept better, cried less, and were happier when they were swaddled. Most babies like being swaddled from their first week of life up until 4-7 weeks from birth. Some babies love swaddling so much, that they are happy to be wrapped for sleep for several months.

There is a bit of an art to swaddling a baby and getting them bundled tightly, but not too tightly. There is a great blanket on the market that makes swaddling effortless. This blanket is called the Miracle Blanket (www.miracleblanket.com) and it makes swaddling easy even if you have a baby who likes to kick a lot.

For people who will be using a regular baby blanket for swaddling, here are the blow-by-blow instructions to a happy well-wrapped baby:

1. Start with a baby blanket that is appropriate for the temperature in the room.

2. Lay the blanket flat- we typically did this on the floor so we didn't have to worry about our babies trying to roll off a table or couch.

3. Fold down one corner of the blanket about 5 inches, this will be the area for your baby's head.

4. Lay your baby down with her head centered on the flipped down corner with the edge of the blanket being at the top of the baby's shoulders.

5. Next, pull one corner of the blanket over the baby, and pull it snug against or just under the baby's side.

6. Flip the bottom of the blanket up to where it covers the baby's feet and body. If it covers her face at all just fold the top corner down. Don't make this fold too tight as you want to give your baby just a bit of room to move her legs.

7. Bring the remaining corner of the blanket across your baby's chest and tuck it underneath your baby. You want this wrap to be snug but not excessively tight.

That's it. After a few days of swaddling you will be able to wrap your baby even in a semi-conscious middle of the night feeding!

The Dirty on Bathing Your Baby

Until your baby's umbilical cord falls off at around two weeks of age, you should clean your baby with a sponge bath. Start by laying your baby on a towel in a warm room. Keep her covered with a blanket or towel, uncovering as you go only the area you are washing. Use a warm wash cloth and mild baby cleanser and then rinse your baby one area at a time. Use cotton balls soaked in warm water to clean around her eyes. Physicians used to recommend the use of rubbing alcohol to clean her umbilical cord but, as of this writing, that practice is no longer deemed necessary by the medical community.

Once the umbilical cord falls off, you can bathe your child in a baby bath. There is little difference between the various baby baths available at most retailers. However, one feature we loved for bathing baby during those early months was the mesh sling attachment that now comes with some baby bathers. It does most of the cradling for you while keeping your baby suspended in water. Fill the bath with warm water between 92°F and 98°F. We used a rubber ducky with a temperature strip so we could be sure of the water's temperature. Place your baby in the bath and use your left hand to hold the baby, while cleaning her with your right. If you don't have a sling attachment for the bath, use a cradling hold—one arm underneath and supporting the baby's head and neck—until your baby is strong enough to support her neck. Babies only a few months old do not need a daily bath, which is too drying for their skin. During the first few months, we bathed our babies every two to three days. If your baby has especially dry or sensitive skin, most pediatricians recommend Dove® Moisturizing Body Wash for Sensitive Skin. You can purchase this at most stores. Look for it in the adult body wash section.

The kitchen sink is a great transition location between an infant bathtub and the full-size bathtub. Once your baby can sit up reliably, you can put her in the sink without a bath accessory. We put a towel down to cover the drain plug, provide traction, and make a cushy place for our babies to sit. Our babies loved this because they had their own little tub complete with a view of the kitchen. We loved it because the height of the kitchen sink is much easier on the back than leaning over a bathtub to give a bath.

Whatever your bathing method or location, never, never, never leave your baby unattended while bathing—not even for a moment.

Don't Waste Time Sterilizing Bottles, Nipples, and Water

I f you are bottle feeding your baby or supplementing breastfeeding with formula, then you will be glad to hear that you don't need to sterilize the bottles, nipples, or the water added to formula. There are two exceptions to this rule: (1) Most nipples, pacifiers, and bottles should be sterilized by boiling water before their first use; and (2) if your water comes from a well, then the American Academy of Pediatrics recommends sterilizing your water before mixing it with formula.

When our son started on formula, we spent countless hours each week sterilizing bottles and nipples. This involved hand washing everything and then boiling each piece in a large pot of water for at least five minutes. It was quite a welcome development when our pediatrician told us that there wasn't any benefit to sterilizing bottles.

Sterilizing bottles was done widely just a decade ago. Many people still believe that sterilization is necessary to keep your baby safe. However, studies done as early as the 1950s show that it is safe to feed infants formula from un-sterilized clean bottles and nipples and city-treated tap water.

One problem you may face, particularly if you have an older dishwasher, is that the dishwasher detergent may leave a film on the nipples and in the bottle. Our son became a difficult eater when we stopped boiling the nipples because our dishwasher was leaving detergent residue on the nipples. We solved this problem by giving the nipples an extra rinse by hand. When we purchased a new home with a new dishwasher, the residue problem disappeared.

Diaper Changing 101

The average baby requires over two thousand diaper changes during her first year of life. You will be surprised at how good you will become at this skill. We changed over five thousand diapers in our first year as parents, and we finally learned some keys to making this dirty job easier.

First, make sure your diaper changing station is fully stocked with supplies: diapers, wipes, diaper rash ointment, a small toy for baby to play with, and a diaper disposal system nearby. Next, place baby down on the changing pad and slide a clean diaper underneath your baby's dirty diaper. Open the dirty diaper and use wipes to clean your baby's bottom. Make sure you clean all of the folds and skin. With girls it is very important to wipe from front to back to avoid spreading fecal matter to the vaginal area. When changing a baby boy, it is a good idea to move quickly or keep his penis covered with a tissue or cloth to avoid a surprise spray.

Once the baby's bottom is clean, pull the dirty diaper out and fold the diaper using the attached tape or Velcro to seal the diaper closed. Rolling the diaper tightly helps to keep the mess and smell inside. Fan your baby's bottom with another diaper to help dry up any moisture. Then, apply diaper rash ointment if needed and fasten the new diaper. Redress your baby and return her to play or bed.

As your baby gets older, having toys nearby will come in handy. We kept special toys that we only allowed our babies to play with during diaper changes. This helped to keep our babies interested and distracted while their diapers were changed.

If your baby is being difficult or is fighting being changed, the best strategy is to distract him by tickling, making a funny face, or any other creative way you may find to distract his attention from the task at hand. Our advice is to be quick and make it fun.

Sleep Through the Night by Twelve Weeks or Sooner

D uring the first few weeks of life with your newborn you may think that your baby will never sleep through the night. However, by following a few guidelines you should be seeing a solid night's sleep before your little angel is twelve weeks old.

There are four keys to making this happen:

1. Put your baby on a consistent schedule

2. Don't use sleep aids, props, or pacifiers (including holding or rocking your baby to sleep)

3. Feed your baby when she wakes up instead of before she goes to sleep

4. Don't respond right away if your baby cries a little (typically less than 5 minutes) when put to bed.

By following these four golden rules, you will be helping your baby learn to fall asleep on her own. If your baby becomes accustomed to getting to sleep through being fed, rocked, or sucking on a pacifier, then she will need these to get back to sleep when she awakens at night. Instead, you want your baby to be able to get herself back to sleep without any parental intervention (which means you get to sleep through the night!). A credible study found that when parents followed these guidelines, eighty-nine percent of babies slept through the night before they were three months old.

If your baby is more than six weeks old and she doesn't show any signs of sleeping through the night, then don't despair. The transition from a nightly waking to a full night's sleep is often very sudden. Each of our four older children suddenly went from needing a nighttime feeding to sleeping the whole night through. Our oldest slept through the night (nine hours of sleep) at 10½ weeks, and our twins, who were 5 weeks premature, slept through the night at 11 weeks, and our fourth child slept through for the first time at 10 weeks, and we have our fingers crossed that our fifth child will follow the same pattern.

You Can't Spoil Your Baby in the First Six Months

L
ike many new parents, we were concerned about how much we could respond to our new baby's cries and needs without spoiling him. The wonderful truth is that you can't spoil your baby by being over-attentive in the first six months. When an infant cries in his first six months, he is expressing a need. He is telling you that he is hungry, his diaper is wet, he is uncomfortable, or that he simply wants you to hold and love him. By responding quickly and effectively to his cries, you help him to establish a sense of trust and comfort.

A major exception to this general rule for responding quickly to your baby's cry is when your baby cries during sleep periods. Most babies partly awaken and cry out at some point during both daytime naps and night sleep. It is important that you only respond when there is something really wrong requiring your assistance (dirty diaper, sickness, etc.). If you are unsure if something is really wrong, then check your baby quickly, preferably without too much playfulness, and then leave the room if everything is alright. Most times your baby will quickly get himself back to sleep. If you respond too quickly and too often when your infant is trying to get back to sleep, you may be disturbing his sleep.

Colic Can Be Treated or Reduced

A baby with colic is one who is healthy and gaining weight, but cries for more than three hours a day for no discernible reason. There is not yet a complete understanding of colic, despite the fact that a tremendous amount of research has been done on the subject. When you are a parent of a baby with colic (we were), you realize what an important issue this to you and your baby.

Surprisingly, twenty to thirty percent of infants suffer from colic. Colic usually peaks at six weeks and then ends when a baby is between four and six months old. In a study of 100 colicky babies, colic disappeared in 50 percent of the babies by three months and 90 percent of the babies at six months of age.

If your baby has signs or symptoms of colic, then see your pediatrician. Colicky babies usually have their crying spells at the same time everyday, typically in the evening. Many babies with colic draw their legs up toward their bellies and clench their fists during a colic episode. Until recently, most pediatricians believed that colic was untreatable. Now pediatricians believe that many instances of colic have a medical cause or can be reduced through specific techniques or medications.

Based on our experience and research, we recommend first switching to a soy formula for a week if you are bottle feeding. A study in 2000 shows that adding lactase to formula or pumped breast milk greatly helps in about twenty-six percent of colic cases. If you are breastfeeding, then reduce as much as possible your consumption of milk, chocolate, onions, and cruciferous vegetables. A 1996 study shows a strong link between previous week's consumption of these foods and colic. You might also try for one week substituting Neocate, an amino acid infant formula without lactose or cow proteins. A 2001 study shows that this change reduced crying and fussing by an average of forty-two percent in five out of six babies. After one week the mothers returned to breast feeding while strictly avoiding milk and dairy products.

A study published in January 2007, recommends treatment with probiotics to help maintain the balance of "good" bacteria in the digestive tract and soothe the colic. Talk to your doctor before administering any medications or change in formulas.

Some breastfed babies cry a great deal because they aren't getting enough to eat. You can test for this by providing a supplemental bottle of pumped breast milk or formula after your baby nurses to see if this reduces or eliminates his crying. If you are bottle-feeding, try Dr. Brown's bottles for a week. Based on parent's feedback, these bottles seem to help by reducing air intake while feeding.

By trial and error, we found activities that helped to soothe our colicky baby. First, try swaddling your baby. This was helpful at first, but stopped working once our baby reached about seven weeks old. Second, lay your baby on his stomach or hold him with his stomach positioned against yours. Holding our baby in this position was particularly helpful after meals. Third, white noise (such as running a vacuum or a fan) or soothing music is often helpful. Many parents and experts report relief when using a baby swing or other rocking motion. Combining these techniques may do the trick for your little one.

Much of the recent literature on colic supports the belief that many cases of colic are actually undiagnosed and untreated cases of reflux. With your pediatrician's assistance, you can determine if reflux may be the cause. Reflux can be accurately diagnosed and is typically treated with prescription medication.

All Diapers are Not Created Equal

There are many choices available when choosing diapers. We recommend that you try several brands and find one that you like. Based on our experience, most diapers work fairly well, but Pampers seems to be slightly better than most. *Consumer Reports* ranks Pampers highest for leak prevention, keeping baby dry, and fastener quality.

Although possibly better for the environment, "green" or environmentally friendly diapers do a poor job of holding in wetness. Cloth diapers, which are used by less than 10 percent of parents, are also less effective at keeping wetness from a baby's skin than are disposable diapers. With the recent trend of "go green," cloth diapers have come a long way. Many new brands are less bulky, can be fastened without pins, and are machine washable. Check out these brands: Adjustable Velcro Diapers by Under the Nile, Bamboo filled Diapers by bumGenius, and Fuzzi Bunz Pocket Diapers.

To save money, the best plan is to buy in bulk and stock up on diapers. Buying a box at a time versus just a package insures that you'll always have diapers available and will get the best deal possible. We found that Target and Wal-Mart offered pricing that was equal to or better than many wholesale stores such as Sam's Club, while grocery stores were typically more expensive.

Circumcision Has No Overall Medical Benefits

Circumcision can be a highly emotional topic for new parents. Male circumcision is an important religious practice for people of Jewish and Muslim faiths. Circumcision was heavily promoted in the United States during Victorian times as a way to reduce the frequency of masturbation.

After extensive studies, the British Health Service discontinued reimbursement for circumcision. In Britain, circumcision is now very rare with less than one percent of British baby boys circumcised. Currently about sixty percent of male children in the United States are circumcised, and the rate of circumcision in the United States continues to fall.

In 1975, the American Academy of Pediatrics' Ad Hoc Task Force Committee on Circumcision declared, "There is no absolute medical indication for routine circumcision of the newborn." Later, the American College of Obstetricians and Gynecologists agreed.

Recent scientific studies show that babies who are circumcised have a slightly lower risk of developing a urinary tract infection during the first years of life and a slightly lower risk of getting sexually transmitted diseases. However, these benefits were not sufficient enough for the American Academy of Pediatrics to recommend circumcision for all boys.

The bottom line is that the choice to have your son circumcised or not is a personal decision. Be aware that there are no significant medical benefits to circumcision but that social and family concerns are yours to consider.

Sometimes Babies Cry to Soothe Themselves

Babies usually cry because they need something. They may be hungry, wet, or wanting attention. However, at times, babies cry simply to soothe themselves. Sometimes a baby becomes over-stimulated by the day's activities and will need to cry to release the stress.

If your baby is crying, do a quick check:

- Is she dry?

- Is it close to time to eat?

- Is her outfit or diaper binding her?

- Is she happy when being held or getting attention?

If these checks don't halt your baby's crying, then your baby may be crying to release stress. Of course, a baby's crying will create stress for you. Determining why your baby is crying, before deciding how to help her, can go a long way in preventing frustration for you and your child.

If your baby is crying to release stress, the best response may be to hold her and let her cry it out, according to developmental psychologist Aletha Solter, PhD:

> Crying often serves the purpose of an important stress-release mechanism for people of all ages, including babies. If your baby refuses to eat and wants to cry instead, she could be expressing a need to cry. Babyhood is very stressful, even with the best of parenting. Perhaps your daughter is trying to release stress from over stimulation or daily frustrations.

This type of crying is particularly common in the early evening. However, if your baby continues to cry for more than 20 or 30 minutes at a time, you may want to review our section on colic: "Colic Can Be Treated or Reduced."

The First Three Months Are the Hardest

We wish someone had told us that the first three months of parenting are the hardest. While we were elated to have a baby, caring for the baby was sometimes physically exhausting.

The first three months are by far the hardest because your baby isn't sleeping through the night yet. A new baby cries frequently and needs to be fed and changed often. In addition, as a new parent you are learning to be a parent and adjusting to a new role and new responsibilities.

Through these first months parents do quite a lot: feeding the baby eight or more times a day, waking up several times a night, changing diapers continually, and all of this with little positive feedback from their babies. At around six to eight weeks of age, most infants will start to smile. The first smile is one of the first signs of your baby's appreciation. As your baby continues to develop, she is able to better express her affection. We found that spending time with our babies was always fun, but became even more rewarding as they developed.

Another important factor is that by the end of three months your baby should be sleeping through the night. This makes a world of difference. As your baby gets older, she will need fewer diaper changes and feedings during the day.

So hold on during those first few months, we promise that parenting gets easier and even better.

The Straight Poop on Diaper Rash

Most babies will endure diaper rash several times in their first year. Yet here is good news: diaper rashes are avoidable and easily treated.

Diaper rash, more common in babies who wear cloth diapers, is caused by moisture in contact with your baby's skin. You prevent diaper rash by cleaning you baby's bottom thoroughly and changing his diapers before they get too wet.

We recommend changing your baby's diaper after each feeding. This ensures at least eight changes a day in the early weeks, when your baby's skin is particularly sensitive.

If your baby develops a rash then treat it immediately. Most diaper rash ointments that contain zinc oxide will work well. You may be surprised by how quickly your baby can heal.

A baby who has diarrhea or is on antibiotics may contract a more challenging diaper rash or an external yeast infection. Our pediatrician recommends treating diaper rashes associated with diarrhea by applying a 50/50 mixture of Maalox liquid and Aquaphor. The Maalox helps to neutralize the acidity of the diarrhea while the Aquaphor protects the skin. When diaper rash hit our house, we would mix up a batch of Maalox and Aquaphor and keep it at our diaper changing station. It is much easier to mix these ingredients if you heat them for about six seconds in a microwave oven at 50 percent power. Make sure the mixture cools before using it on your baby.

If a rash lasts more than one or two days and resists regular diaper ointment, then it is likely caused by a yeast infection. A yeast infection rash has small white rings or small blister-like pustules. This type of rash can be effectively treated with over the counter anti-fungal medicines such as Lotrimin AF. After applying the anti-fungal medicine, you should see improvement within twenty-four hours of treatment. Always check with your doctor if your baby's diaper rash persists for more than a few days or if it is not responsive to home treatment.

When to Burp Your Baby

I f you bottle feed, your doctor or hospital staff member may tell you to burp your baby after every one-half to one ounce during the first few weeks. Once your baby's digestive system matures at about four weeks, you can burp him less often. We found that it works well to burp a baby every one-third of a bottle. For example, if your baby is eating six ounces per feeding, then burp him after every two ounces. Breast-fed babies will need to be burped less frequently, and some breast-fed babies may not need to be burped at all, because a baby usually takes in little or no air when breastfeeding.

Some babies tell you when they need to burp by taking a break from eating or by beginning to fuss or cry. Unfortunately, many babies don't provide these warning signs. By the time a baby is crying, he has a lot of gas that is making him uncomfortable. It is easier on your baby if you burp him before the pressure from excess gas becomes too painful.

As your baby grows older and his digestive system matures, he will need to be burped even less often while feeding. We found that at about six months of age, our babies didn't need to be burped anymore. They burped on their own at the end of the feeding because they were sitting up and moving around.

Crying Peaks at Six Weeks and Then Declines

Although the sound of an infant crying can tug at your heartstrings and deafen your hearing, crying is very natural during the first six weeks of life. The average baby's crying will peak at six weeks of age—when crying can occur for almost three hours a day! The good news is that the crying will drop off quickly. By six months of age most babies cry less than one hour per day.

The chart below shows the average number of hours infants cry in their first three months.

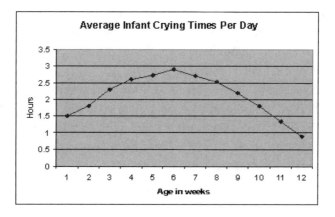

When Should My Baby Nap and Sleep?

Quality sleep is very important for your baby's development and disposition.

Newborns typically sleep between 16 and 20 hours a day, broken up into eight or nine naps. For the first month, your baby will typically eat, stay awake a few minutes, and then sleep again. In her second month, she will nap about six times during the day and sleep a longer session or two at night. Starting in the third month, your baby may sleep seven to nine hours at night and take four naps of 1½ to 2 hours during the day.

At six to nine months, most babies will sleep about 11 hours at night and take a morning and afternoon nap, each nap lasting 1½ to 2 hours. Many babies will also need a late-afternoon or early-evening nap.

This sleep pattern remains consistent until one year of age. At the end of this book we provide the schedules we used with our children.

Use a Carrier, Sling, or Wrap to Stay Close to Baby

Infant carriers and slings allow you to be physically close to your baby and keep your hands free. We enjoyed being physically close during the day, and our babies seemed to love snuggling with mom or dad. Many studies show that babies carried close to their mother much of the day cry a great deal less. In addition, carrying the extra weight can be good exercise!

While slings can be used without regard to weight and height minimums, you should not use a baby carrier for babies weighing less than eight pounds and/or less than 21 inches long.

There are many brands of child carriers and slings, most of which do a fine job. The carrier we found to be most comfortable and stylish for a child under 24 pounds is the City Carrier by Baby Björn. Take the time to adjust and fit the carrier correctly so that it remains comfortable during an extended outing. If you find the carrier uncomfortable or tiring, especially in your shoulders or lower back, adjust the straps until you get a good fit.

Most carriers are designed to be worn with your baby facing your chest until your baby's neck is sufficiently strong, typically at about two months of age. Once your baby can hold her head up by herself, she can face forward and get a great view of the world.

When our fourth child was born, we used the opportunity to try out several slings. After lots of research, we fell in love with the fleece sling by Hotslings®. Not only are the slings comfortable for both wearer and baby, but they are stylish too! Slings generally can be used in a cradle position with young infants and transition to a side-hip position as your baby matures. We liked our slings so much that we used a sling with our fourth child until she was two.

On the advice of countless mothers, we bought a Moby Wrap® to use with our fifth child. As of this writing, our baby is only weeks old, but we love the comfort and convenience of the Moby Wrap®. It was a bit confusing to use at first, but we quickly got the hang of it. With our four other children to chase around, having two hands free is invaluable. Although we still use the sling, the wrap is the most comfortable of all our baby carriers.

How Much Should My Baby Eat?

L ike many parents, we often wondered if our baby was eating the right amount of food. While every baby is different, the following chart sets forth the average food and liquid consumption during the first year.

Baby's Age	Servings of Food Daily	Average Amount of Formula or Breastfeeding
Newborn	None	16-24 oz. of formula OR Breastfeeding 8 to 12 times a day
1 month	None	24-36 oz. of formula OR Breastfeeding 8 to 9 times a day
2 months	None	24-42 oz. of formula OR Breastfeeding 6 to 9 times a day
3 to 6 months	None	28-48 oz. of formula OR Breastfeeding 6 to 8 times a day
6 to 9 months	2 fruits 2 vegetables 1-2 cereals 1-2 meats	24-36 oz. of formula OR Breastfeeding 4 to 6 times a day
9 to 12 months	2 fruits 2 vegetables 2 cereals 1-2 meats	24-32 oz. of formula OR Breastfeeding 3 to 4 times a day

It is important to understand just how small a "serving" is for your baby. For vegetables, fruit, and meat, one serving equals only one to three tablespoons, which is not very much. For instance, five cut up green beans is one serving. Many parents are concerned that their baby is not eating enough, because it is easy to forget how much smaller a serving size is for a baby than for an adult.

Don't worry if the amount your baby eats on any particular day varies. Several studies show that the amount babies will typically eat varies by as much as thirty percent from day to day. Like adults, babies have days they are more or less hungry.

Ideas for Dressing Your Newborn

The outfits for newborn babies are so cute! But, save your money until your baby is at least two months old. Your newborn will spend most of her time in onesies and pajamas.

Newborn babies sleep, eat, spit-up, and dirty diapers frequently. These messy activities call for comfortable and easily washable clothing. We recommend buying several one-piece pajamas with footies or gown-type pajamas with elastic around the bottom. Pajamas that snap closed are more convenient than pajamas that zip all the way up. Zippered one-piece outfits have to be unzipped entirely for diaper changing, leaving a baby uncovered and cold. We especially liked gowns for quick and easy middle-of-the-night diaper changes.

Once your baby is two months old and spending more time awake, dressing your baby can become a fun morning activity that signals to her that the day is beginning. We suggest buying comfortable, soft clothes that are non-binding and loose-fitting, allowing room to grow.

Save Your Money on Crib Bumpers and Quilts

L
ike most new parents, you probably shopped and shopped until you found the perfect crib ensemble that includes a crib bumper and quilt for your baby. Before you spend the money, we recommend putting the bumper and the quilt back.

Crib bumpers are an American invention not typically used elsewhere. Bumpers serve very little purpose and can actually become a safety risk for your baby. Bumpers are sold as a safety device to protect your baby's head from hitting the side rails of the crib. The truth is that when your bay is first born, she usually won't move much in her crib.

If you do use a bumper, be sure that the pad goes all the way around the crib and is secured with at least six straps or ties that keep the bumper from falling in from the sides. For safety reasons, the ties should be no more than six inches long.

A number of groups including the American Academy of Pediatrics have issued warnings about the danger of crib bumpers when a baby is able to sit or stand. As soon as your baby can pull up to a standing position, remove your crib bumper along and any toys or stuffed animals that a baby could use as a step for climbing out.

Like bumpers, quilts are not necessary during your baby's first year. Babies should not have blankets, particularly thick ones, in their cribs before they are at least six months old. Blankets increase the likelihood of sudden infant death syndrome (SIDS). This means that quilts are not useful and may actually be dangerous. Nearly every mother we spoke with felt like she wasted money on the matching quilt because her baby never used it. Don't worry; you will have plenty of other places to spend your money—like saving for college tuition! If you have already have a quilt, you can hang it on a wall in your baby's room or place it next to your rocker for cuddling during late-night feedings.

Breastfeeding Can Be a Challenge

Breastfeeding your baby is a wonderful gift and a special bonding experience. Like all things in life, great success usually comes with great effort, and breastfeeding is no exception. Your new baby is born with a suck reflex, but doesn't know how to latch on and breastfeed. Just as you will be learning to feed your baby, he will be learning how to feed himself. Most mothers report that the first six weeks of breastfeeding are very challenging and require a real commitment.

There are many benefits to breastfeeding. If you and your baby enjoy the experience, it is truly worth the time and effort. For expert advice, speak with the lactation consultants and nursing staff while you are still in the hospital. Even after you leave, most hospitals offer telephone lactation consultations free of charge to their patients. The leading proponent of breastfeeding, the La Leche League, is a great resource and offers much valuable breastfeeding information (http://www.lalecheleague.org).

Our advice is to be mentally prepared for some bumps in the road as you breastfeed. Remember that both you and your baby are learning a new skill together. If you get frustrated, use the experts and try again. If, despite your best efforts, breastfeeding doesn't work for you then don't feel guilty about switching to bottle-feeding.

There Are Few "Perfect" Births

M any women imagine a perfect birth for themselves and their children. Yet many new mothers are disappointed that their birth experience was not as positive or perfect as they had hoped. While difficulties in delivery cannot be avoided, regrets about these difficulties can.

The delivery of our twins was not at all how we had envisioned it. They were delivered by emergency cesarean section. We had hoped for a vaginal birth with no complications and instead faced major surgery with life-threatening complications. At first we were disappointed that "our moment" wasn't what we had hoped for. Soon though, we realized that our birth was "perfect" for us. It resulted in the birth of our two healthy babies, and that is about as perfect as it can get.

If you were disappointed in how your delivery turned out, then it is important to leave this experience behind and be grateful for your health and your new child. Every baby's birth is a miracle.

Let Your Baby Sleep Alone

B abies are warm and cuddly, and it is very natural to want your little angel to sleep next to you at night. This leads many parents to sleep with their babies in the same bed or room with them. We tried this for a short while with our first child and found that it was not a good idea for us. Not only did the quality of our sleep suffer, but also we lost important couple time.

Although some families are able to make it work, we believe that for most families sleeping with your baby is not a good idea for several reasons. Sleeping with your baby will most likely result in less sleep for both you and your baby. The noises baby makes can keep you awake and you will probably respond to little cries and whimpers that might otherwise not be heard or warrant a response. Co-sleeping may also delay teaching her to learn to sleep on her own. This can cause a difficult struggle when you want your baby to start sleeping in her own bed or her own room. In addition, there are several studies that show a higher likelihood of sudden infant death syndrome (SIDS) when children sleep in the same bed with their parents. The likelihood is particularly dangerous if the parents drink or smoke.

According to the U.S. National Institute of Health (NIH),

> There are some reports of infants being suffocated by overlying by an adult... Co-sleeping on sofas has emerged as a major risk factor in one study. Others studies have shown bed sharing with multiple family members in an adult bed to be particularly hazardous for the infant.

In addition, co-sleeping may reduce the quality of sleep for your newborn. According to the NIH, "Some behavioral studies have demonstrated that infants have more arousals and less slow-wave sleep during bed sharing." Experts believe this slow-wave sleep is essential for your baby's proper brain development.

We realize that the decision of where baby will sleep is a personal one and can be emotionally charged for some people. If you decide to have your baby sleep with you, then don't second guess your choice. Many parents successfully sleep with their babies in the baby's early months. And, in many cultures it is perfectly normal and natural for newborns to sleep with the parents.

Don't Buy Special Baby Laundry Detergent

There are several brands of "infant" laundry detergent on the market. The premise of these special detergents is that a baby's sensitive skin may be irritated by clothing that is washed in regular laundry detergents that contain perfumes and dyes. The downside is that these special baby detergents, such as Dreft, cost approximately twice as much as regular brand name detergents.

Most major detergent brands now offer varieties of detergent with no bleach, dyes, or fragrances so there is no longer a need to buy a separate baby detergent. Both Tide and Cheer come in varieties called "Tide Free" and "Cheer Free" respectively. Tide and Cheer are highly rated by *Consumer Reports* in a review of laundry detergents. Another added benefit is that you can wash all of your family's laundry mixed in with baby's clothes. There will be no need to wash a separate load of baby clothes with special baby laundry detergent. You will save money and probably find that these detergents do a great job at cleaning your infant's dirty clothing.

If you use fabric softener or dryer sheets, be sure you use products that are dye-free and fragrance-free. You can usually switch back to regular-scented detergent once your baby is one year old. If your baby has sensitive skin, you may want to wait a bit longer. If, after switching, you notice a rash or other irritation on your baby's skin, go back to the "free" varieties for a while longer and consult your pediatrician.

Breaks from Parenting Are Important

Taking care of a newborn infant makes it easy to lose perspective and sleep. While we don't have an easy solution for the lack of sleep, we have learned that regular breaks from childcare responsibilities are important. We recommend making sure that you have at least one break from your baby every week. If you can manage it, a break of just two or three hours is extremely beneficial, although a half day or more is even better.

There are two keys to making sure these breaks truly restore you. First, have someone you really trust watching your baby while you are gone. Ask your spouse, the baby's grandparent, another relative, or maybe a babysitter. If you don't have this confidence, you won't be able to take a true mental break from the hard work of infant care.

At the end of this book, you will find a sample Guide for Babysitters. We used our Guide for Babysitters as a one-stop resource for any and all the information anyone would need to take care of our babies while we were gone. Knowing that our babysitter had access to this information was a stress reliever for us and valuable resource for our caregiver.

Second, to make the time truly restorative, you should go out and spend time alone or with your spouse, family, or friends. This can be eating lunch at a restaurant, drinking coffee at a café, browsing a bookstore, shopping at the mall, reading at the library, or whatever you find to be relaxing. What you do doesn't matter; what is important is getting a physical and mental break from taking care of your baby.

Many parents feel selfish taking this time for themselves. DON'T! This regular break will make you a better parent by reducing your stress and restoring your sense of perspective. We guarantee that you will return home refreshed and ready to take care of your little angel.

It is Often Difficult to Tell What Your Baby's Cry Means

Often your baby will cry and you will know immediately exactly what is wrong. Equally often, you will not easily recognize what the cry means.

Most studies of crying demonstrate that you can't decipher a baby's message based on the sound of her cry. Studies using both mothers and experienced neonatal nurses show that neither group can accurately identify more than fifty percent of the time, based only on listening to a baby's cry, why the baby is crying.

So, you shouldn't feel like you aren't a good parent if you can't decipher your baby's cry every time. Instead, do a quick assessment. Is she wet? Is her diaper on too tight? Does she suck on your finger when you put it in her mouth indicating that she is hungry? Did she stop crying when you picked her up? Our best advice is to pay close attention to your baby and her schedule to get a feel for what she typically needs at different times of the day. By quickly discovering your child's needs, you can help her to relax by effectively meeting her needs.

Don't Worry about Baby Acne

During your baby's first months, she may suffer from baby acne. While you may worry, or even be embarrassed, that your baby's complexion is less than perfect, the good news is that this condition is nothing to worry about and will usually clear up on its own after a few months.

Baby acne is typically caused by excess hormones that a baby receives from her mother before she is born. It can take up to four months for the effect of these hormones to be completely eliminated from a baby's system. Fortunately, this temporary condition will have no long-term effects on your baby's complexion. In addition, there is little, if any, correlation between baby acne and the acne a child may develop during adolescence.

During the early months, treat baby acne by washing your baby's face with water and mild baby soap and applying a small amount of one-percent hydrocortisone cream. If your baby's acne is severe or doesn't improve considerably by three months of age, then her acne may have other causes.

Recent research shows that most severe cases of baby acne are caused by a type of yeast. If acne is caused by a yeast infection, it can be treated with an over-the-counter anti-fungal medicine such as Lotrimin AF, and should clear up within a couple of weeks of treatment. If your baby's complexion hasn't cleared up by six months of age, we recommend taking her to see a dermatologist for evaluation and treatment.

Put Your Baby to Bed Awake

This simple key is an absolute essential to helping your baby develop good sleep habits. Many parents and caregivers enjoy holding, nursing, or rocking their baby to sleep. This is enjoyable for the parent, but helping your baby fall asleep is not a good idea in the long run. Many parents spend hours every night getting their children to bed because the children have become accustomed to having a parent's help getting to sleep.

As we mention in our section about sleep paradoxes (later in the book), sleep is a skill that your baby needs to learn. Just as throwing a ball for your child doesn't teach him how to throw the ball, getting your child to sleep by rocking, nursing, or pacifying him does not allow him to learn how to get himself to sleep.

We can't overstress the importance of good sleep habits for your baby. Good sleep habits are important not only for your child but also for the happy functioning of your family. A baby that wakes up at night usually disrupts the entire family's sleep. Babies that can't fall asleep on their own also tend to be unable to go back to sleep on their own when they awaken at night. Studies show that babies who don't get enough sleep have shorter attention spans, don't learn as well, and have disruptive behavior. Some studies show that poor sleep habits formed during infancy can continue into adolescence and adulthood.

Putting your baby down for a nap or at bedtime when he is awake shouldn't be difficult. Put him in his crib, give him a kiss and say goodnight. Leave the room. Going to bed should not be a big production—be loving, but don't linger. If you hear him fussing or crying, don't return for at least five minutes. If you do need to return, reassure him that you are just outside the room and tell your baby that it is time to go to sleep. Leave again. Repeat as necessary. This skill should only take a few days to learn. Even the most difficult sleepers will usually improve within a week. If you start putting your baby to bed awake when he is first born, your baby will learn from birth how to comfort himself and go to sleep on his own. This is a wonderful skill for him to have for life!

Breastfeeding Is Best, Formulas with ARA and DHA Are Best for the Rest

E xperts agree that the best option for your baby is breast-feeding. However, there are many people who can not or choose not to breastfeed for a variety of reasons. If you are going to feed your baby formula, then we recommend using a formula that includes the essential fatty acids ARA (arachidonic acid) and DHA (docosahexaenoic acid).

Recent studies show that mental development and visual acuity improve in infants who drink formula with ARA and DHA. Studies showing only minimal benefits from these fatty acids use different methodologies and lower amounts of ARA and DHA than studies that reveal the positive effects of these acids. In addition, a recent study shows that mothers who consume higher-than-normal amounts of DHA during pregnancy have babies who sleep better than other babies in their first year of life.

These essential fatty acids have been added to infant formulas in over sixty other countries. Although a newborn baby is unable to produce sufficient quantities of these fatty acids, only within the last few years have these nutrients been approved for use in the United States. Studies show no negative effects of adding ARA and DHA to formula.

The two largest manufacturers of infant formula in the US— Ross Products (producer of Similac) and Mead Johnson (producer of Enfamil)—both now offer formulas supplemented with ARA and DHA. Talk to your pediatrician before making any formula switch, then look for these new formulas marketed as Similac Advance and Enfamil Lipil.

Put Your Marriage/Partner First

Keep your marriage and partner a top priority during your baby's first year of life. As new parents we know how difficult this can be. It is easy to become so caught up in taking care of the new baby that you don't spend time keeping your relationship strong. By making your partner a priority, you are building a stronger family for your child. By making central the relationship with your spouse, you provide an excellent role model of what a loving relationship should be.

Someday your child will leave your home, and if she has always been the center of the universe at home, it will be difficult for her to adjust. Similarly, if you and your spouse put all of your energy into raising your children, you may find yourselves lost when it comes to resuming your role as a married couple alone at home again.

We recommend setting a date night at least once a month. Arrange for a trusted relative or babysitter to watch your little one and go have dinner together. If money is an issue, do something inexpensive, but do it together. The point here is to spend time together as a couple. As your baby gets a little older, consider making your date night an every week or every other week affair. While the first time out without our baby was difficult, we quickly learned to treasure our time together. We now schedule a date night at least every other week and look forward to our time together.

Don't Isolate Your Baby from Noise While Sleeping

Teaching your baby from the very beginning to sleep in the same conditions that she will encounter as she gets older is important. If you keep it very quiet every time your baby sleeps, your baby will become conditioned to a very quiet sleep atmosphere. This means that your baby will be much more sensitive to noises when they do occur. We found that the best strategy is to go about your normal routine when baby is napping: run the vacuum, move about the house, make your regular phone calls. This will teach your baby to tune out normal noises and sleep soundly.

This worked so well for us that one of our twins can be completely asleep while the other is crying only six feet away! If you follow this advice, you won't have to be afraid that your baby will awaken if the phone rings or someone knocks on your door while your baby is sleeping, which from our experience will happen quite frequently.

Hang a Mobile over the Crib

O ne of the best early developmental toys you should pur-chase is a mobile to hang above your baby's crib. At birth, your baby is drawn to bold contours because his sight is not very acute. Research reveals that most babies can see the color red at birth, but the ability to distinguish green, blue, and yellow doesn't develop until one month of age. By two months of age your baby will be able to see colors and will best focus on objects that are twelve to eighteen inches away. By three months, your baby's abil-ity to focus and track will cause him to really enjoy watching a col-orful, moving mobile. You should change the objects to give your baby variety and to keep up with his improving vision. In addition, a moving mobile will help your baby to develop his skills at track-ing moving objects.

Most authorities recommend taking down the mobile once baby can sit up, because a mobile could then create a safety haz-ard. We found that our children enjoyed their mobiles until they were between seven and nine months old.

Once your baby is old enough to move about his crib, you may want to put one or two small toys and a few board books in your baby's crib. This will offer him something to play with quietly when he first awakens. Rotate the toys and books in your baby's crib every two or three weeks so that your baby always has new and interesting items to play with.

Make Diaper Smells Disappear with a Diaper Genie

E ven though she smells like heaven when she's fresh out of the bath, your baby will make some very smelly diapers during her first year. Most parents want to dispose of baby's diapers without any lingering odors. Although nothing completely eliminates the smell, we found that the Diaper Genie is durable and does the best job of keeping diaper smells contained. It works by sealing each individual diaper. We also liked the Safety 1st Neat!® Diaper Disposal System and the Daiper Genie II. They work on the same principle as the Diaper Genie except there is not any twisting required making them a bit easier to operate.

One of the drawbacks of both the Diaper Genie and the Neat! is that they each use proprietary bags that cost about five dollars per package. Each refill holds about 140 newborn diapers or 95 large diapers. If you put every diaper in the Daiper Genie, the refill should last about three weeks. The other disadvantage is that changing the bags requires a little practice at first.

We recommend spraying your diaper disposal container at least once a month with a disinfectant spray, such as Lysol, and then leaving it open outside to air out. We also gave our Diaper Genie a thorough cleaning every couple of months to kill germs and eliminate lingering odors.

From our experience, none of the other diaper pail products are able to contain diaper smells adequately. We tried throwing our diapers directly into our outside trash. While this worked fine in the winter months, in the summer it smelled terrible and attracted many flies. So, despite the cost and a little added complexity, we highly recommend a Diaper Genie to keep diaper odor under control.

Accept Your Baby for Who He Is

Every baby is born with his or her own distinct temperament and personality. Within two months of your baby's birth, you should start to see some of his inborn personality traits starting to emerge. While some parents mesh perfectly with their offspring, others find any personality differences unsettling.

How well a parent's hopes, dreams, expectations, and ambitions for a child match the child's actual talent and temperament is a major factor in how easy it will be to parent a baby. If you are constantly disappointed with your baby, or wish that he were different, your baby will easily sense this and believe that there is something wrong with him.

It is not your baby's job to mold himself to your expectations. Once your baby is born, it is time to throw out your expectations and love and accept your baby for who he or she is.

Dr. Spock described how well a baby's personality matched a parent's expectations as "goodness of fit." According to Dr. Spock:

> ... [I]n my experience, it is goodness-of-fit issues that seem to cause the most discipline and other problems for parents... If you can learn to accept and love your child for who he really is (and not what you would like him to be) then your life together is likely to be a lot smoother.

If you find yourself parenting a baby who is different than the child you dreamed of, accept the baby you have and learn to love him for who he is.

Feeding Solids Will Not Make Your Baby Sleep Through the Night

Many parents rush their babies into eating solid foods because they mistakenly believe that this will help their little ones sleep through the nigh sooner or sleep longer at night. Studies consistently show that eating solid foods does not improve an infant's ability to sleep at night. Introducing solids too early can have negative consequences.

Introducing solid foods too early also may:

- decrease the baby's intake of breast milk or formula, both of which are nutritionally preferable to solid foods

- reduce the absorption of nutrients such as iron from the intestinal tract

- increase the risk for potentially serious allergic reactions

- cause problems with constipation, diarrhea, or intestinal gas

In addition, solid foods are messy, increase your laundry volume, and are inconvenient to feed on the go.

While some friends or relatives may encourage you to start feeding solids at four months of age, most parents find that it is a lot less work to wait and start infants on solids when they are closer to six months old. We introduced solid foods to our first baby at four months of age and found it took him at least six weeks to begin eating well. A friend of ours summed it up best, "I might as well have waited till my baby was six months old before feeding solid food because it took her almost two months to learn how to eat reasonably well."

You Can't Have Too Many Burp Rags

***

You can never have too many burp rags. Okay, maybe you can have too many, but we seriously found these little rectangles of cloth to be a valuable commodity. Infants spit up, drool, and make messes so frequently that it is a good idea to have a large supply of burp rags available. We used them as emergency bibs, changing pads, bottle props, blankets, and of course as clothing protectors.

We recommend buying at least fifteen burp rags for your baby. That way when you are behind on the laundry you will still have some clean burp rags available. Also, be sure to use the burp rag to protect your clothing every time you hold or burp your baby after feeding. Babies seem to have a sixth-sense about spitting up whenever there is unprotected clothing in range.

The Paradoxes of Sleep

Infants tire and sleep differently than adults. As adults, the more tired we become, the more we want to sleep. However, baby's sleep habits don't work the same way. Instead, as a baby becomes more tired, it often becomes more difficult for her to fall asleep. Sleep-deprived babies become overtired, making it very difficult for them to get to sleep. In addition to having a difficult time achieving sleep, an overtired baby will sleep less deeply and is more likely to wake in the middle of a nap or during the night.

Although it seems like a new baby can sleep anytime or anywhere, as your baby becomes more alert, her sleep pattern becomes more important. There is actually a small window of time between putting your baby down to sleep successfully and having her struggle to achieve sleep. We recommend two tips for getting your little angel into blissful slumber: (1) a flexible but consistent schedule, and (2) an awareness of sleep cues. Typical sleepy signs include: eye rubbing, staring into space, yawning, and being fussy. If it is close to her normal nap or bedtime and your baby shows any of these sleep signs, then it is best to put your baby down to bed with little delay.

Another surprising situation is that when a baby doesn't get her normal amount of sleep during the day, she will usually sleep less well at night. Because of this, if you want your infant to sleep well during the night, then it is very important that she get good naps during the day. After one month of age, you should keep the times and the length of your baby's naps as consistent as possible. As your baby gets older, she may play in her crib for a while before going to sleep. This is normal and doesn't mean that she needs less sleep. Continue with your schedule and be consistent. Nearly all babies benefit from stability in their schedules, particularly in the area of sleep.

Tummy Time Is Terrific

Because of the tremendous concern and publicity regarding sudden infant death syndrome (SIDS), many babies spend little or no time lying on their stomachs. This is unfortunate because the time an infant spends on his tummy helps develop shoulder and arm strength; decreases the chance of developing a flattened or irregular shaped head, and promotes crawling and rolling skills.

In order to provide tummy time and still protect your baby from SIDS, we recommend starting at around two months of age, placing your baby on her stomach for a short period of time during each awake cycle. At first she may only be able to tolerate it for a minute or two, but she will soon be comfortable being on her stomach for longer periods of time. You can increase your baby's enjoyment of her tummy time by varying her views and by placing toys both within and just outside of her reach. Another tip is to take a rolled up bath towel or a nursing pillow and place it under baby's arms. This will prop her up expanding her view of the world.

Tips for Parents of Multiples

I f you are expecting more than one baby or just delivered twins, triplets or more, congratulations and welcome to life with multiples! While we were originally concerned that we might not be able to have children, we ended up being blessed with the birth of our twins within the same year that our first child was born. It was exciting, but scary and overwhelming at times. We were lucky to be tapped into several great networks of parents with multiples and were privy to much needed advice and experience from these amazing parents.

If you recently found out that you are carrying multiples it is important to be sure to be gaining weight as early as possible in your pregnancy. Adequate nutrition and weight gain in the early stages of your pregnancy are particularly helpful in ensuring that your babies are likely to make it close to full term. Mothers of multiples are more likely to suffer from preeclampsia, so this is something that your obstetrician should be on the lookout for. If you have excessively swollen feet and/or ankles this is a strong sign that you may be suffering from preeclampsia. Some doctors believe that the risk of preeclampsia can be reduced by including extra Omega 3 oils (typically flaxseed or fish oil) to your diet. Since these oils are also linked to better vision and brain development it is a wise precaution to make sure you are taking high quality fish oil omega 3 supplements. As always, check with your physician before taking any medication or over the counter product while pregnant.

We recommend preparing as much as possible in advance. There is a good chance that your babies will not make it to full term before delivering, so getting everything ready extra early is a good plan. Once the babies arrive, accept any extra help that you can. If you have friends or relatives that offer to help with the babies, say yes to their help. There will be plenty of work to be done and other mothers often love the opportunity to take care of a newborn again. We recommend that you keep a notebook with offers and what people are willing to do. If you go on bed rest or have a difficult delivery these helpers will be particularly important.

If you can find someone to help take care of some of the overnight duties it can be a lifesaver. We were fortunate to find a college student working on her nursing degree who came to our house two nights a week from 10pm until 6am when our twins were just weeks old. It provided her some extra cash and gave us a much needed night of sleep. If you are breastfeeding, you will still need to get up once during the middle of night to feed the babies or pump to keep your milk supply strong. If your babies have any medical issues or if you can afford a higher cost, there are firms that will provide a trained nurse overnight. These nurses will usually perform extra services such as laundry or light cleaning while the babies are sleeping.

Buying two, three or four of everything is usually not necessary. However there are a number of supplies that you will need to have on hand, these include:

1) An infant car seat for each baby

2) Lots and lots of diapers (calculate at least eight per day per baby)

3) If you are using formula, then plenty of bottles and formula (enough to get through one full day)

4) A twin, triplet or quad stroller or jogger for outings

5) A crib for each baby (we initially slept our babies in the same bassinet and then the same crib but needed to separate them

when they grew too big to share the space any longer at about four months)

As soon as possible after coming home with the babies, we highly recommend putting the babies on the same sleeping and eating schedule. Feed them at the same time, put them down at the same time and get them up at the same time. We've spoken with many, many mothers of multiples and this is almost always the top piece of advice that other multiple moms offer. In fact, we've noticed that mothers of multiples are much more likely to use a consistent daily schedule with their babies. A schedule helps create predictability and order in what can be a turbulent time.

Our final recommendation is to join a twins or multiples group in your local area. There are over 400 local organizations for mothers of twins and multiples. The National Organization of Mothers of Twins Clubs offers information and a search function for local clubs at nomotc.org. It is tremendously helpful to get tips, discuss parenting challenges, and just know that you aren't the only one going through the challenges of parenting multiples. In addition, many of the clubs offer some good ways to save money such as annual or biannual twin clothing and equipment sales.

Spitting Up Is Normal

S pitting up is completely normal and should not be a cause of concern. Many infants spit up after they eat. Because a baby's throat and digestive system are still maturing, most babies will frequently spit up between feedings. Spitting up usually completely stops, or is greatly reduced, around six months of age.

However, if your child is throwing up forcefully—that is, material shoots a few inches out of the baby's mouth—then you should consult your doctor. If this hasn't happened before, then the cause is most likely a virus or infection. However, there are potentially more serious causes, such as an obstruction in the intestines or other diseases. You should call your pediatrician immediately if your baby's vomiting is accompanied by listlessness, poor eating, fever, or if her vomit includes blood.

Drop the Mylicon Drops

A baby who fusses frequently during nursing or bottle-feeding may be suffering from excess gas. This eating-associated fussy behavior is especially true of babies with colic or colic-like symptoms. The natural and logical thought is that if the infant's gas can be reduced or eliminated, then she will feel better.

Mylicon drops, with the active ingredient symethicone, are an over-the-counter drug marketed to help reduce an infant's gas. While some people believe that Mylicon drops make a difference, we found that they failed to help despite trying them countless times. Recent research shows that symethicone is not effective in reducing colic or helping to reduce the amount of time a baby cries. So, we recommend not wasting your time and money giving your baby symethicone for gas pain.

So what do you do to eliminate gas and gas pain in your little angel? Burp your baby! It sounds simple, but don't underestimate the positive effects of helping your baby burp. Four of our children would stop nursing or drinking from their bottles until we sat them upright and helped them to burp. Sometimes burping will take up to five minutes, but once a burp is out your baby will definitely be happier.

If you are bottle-feeding and your baby has gas or colic symptoms, you may want to try Dr. Brown's bottles. These bottles, which have a very loyal following by parents of babies with colic, are specifically designed to prevent air from getting into baby's tummy. When everything else failed, we used Dr. Brown's bottles with one of our daughters. We were very happy to find that feeding her with these bottles greatly reduced her gas pain and discomfort.

Don't Over-Stimulate Your Baby

While your baby needs love and attention, there is a limit to the amount of stimulation that he can handle. During each of his awake times throughout the day, he should have some time that is stimulating and some time that is relaxing. During your baby's first three months, he will be bombarded by stimuli because his senses haven't developed enough to block out the extraneous sounds and lights that he will eventually learn to ignore. Because of this, giving him some time in a relatively quiet room without a lot going on can be soothing.

You may notice that your baby is fussier after he is held by strangers or by several different people in a row. This may be particularly noticeable during family gatherings. If your baby is fussy during these times then it is often his attempt to tell you that he has had enough stimulation. If your baby has become over-stimulated then the best solution is to put him in a quiet and less brightly lit area for a while. Also, putting him in a baby swing will often help calm him.

Let Your Baby Cry Himself to Sleep

F or most babies a little crying prior to falling asleep is perfectly normal. Some babies will start to cry or fuss when they become tired, indicating their need for sleep. If your baby is on a schedule and it is close to his normal nap or bed time, then your baby's excessive whining or crying is likely his way of telling you that he is ready for sleep.

Don't worry if your baby cries for a few minutes before going to sleep, this is a normal part of winding down for many babies. The amount of crying a baby does before falling asleep varies a great deal. For instance, one of our sons seldom cried before going to sleep, while one of our daughters cried for about three minutes every time she was put to bed.

It's best to leave your baby alone and only check on him if he cries for more than five minutes. Although leaving a baby alone while he is crying is difficult, it is a very important lesson for teaching your baby to learn to self-sooth and sleep on his own.

Talk, Talk, and More Talk

Every parent looks forward to the first time his or her baby utters "Mama" or "Dada." So it is natural for parents to wonder about the best way to help their baby develop verbal skills. Research shows that the most effective means of helping your baby develop his language skills is to talk to him often. For instance, tell him what you are doing when you are changing him or feeding him. Tell him about the things that you see when you take him on a walk. Speaking in baby talk—that is, speaking slowly with a sing-song quality—comes naturally to most parents and helps your baby to understand language more easily during those early months.

According to Dorothy Dougherty, author of *How To Talk To Your Baby*, "Research tells us that the more words babies hear, the faster they learn to talk. This is because frequent daily exposure to words helps the brain pathways that foster language learning to develop more fully. However, only 'live' language, not television, helps children develop language skills."

Play Music for Your Baby

B abies love music. Some research shows that listening to music may help develop spatial, mathematical, and higher reasoning skills. Although some recent studies call into question this so-called "Mozart Effect," several studies suggest that playing an instrument is helpful in developing mathematical abilities. If your child is exposed to music when he is young, he may be more likely to want to sing or learn an instrument as he grows older.

We recommend playing a variety of music to your children. Our babies seem to enjoy almost all the music that we play, whether classical, country, rock, or oldies. Also, babies that are three months and younger can hear sounds while sleeping. So feel free to play music to your newborn during naps.

A few CDs that are calming and make for great background music while playing with your baby are:

- Mozart in the Morning (our favorite)

- Build Your Baby's Brain

- Baby's First Mozart

As your baby grows older, you may want to play music at bedtime to calm him and signal that sleep time has arrived. In addition to the music listed above, we made each of our children their very own bedtime CD with some of our favorite relaxing songs.

Know When to Call Your Pediatrician

The typical infant will be sick between three and nine times in his first year. Many of these illnesses will occur from a cold virus and won't require any attention from your pediatrician. Low grade fevers, or those less than 101°F, are usually harmless and can be the result of a minor virus or teething. If the low fever continues more than three days, call your physician. However, anytime your baby has a fever over 101°F, you should call your pediatrician right away to discuss your baby's condition.

Be especially watchful during the first few months of your baby's life, when a fever or any illness should be brought to your doctor's attention immediately. While most illnesses will not be anything serious, a fever can be a sign of an infection. One of the biggest risks is bacterial meningitis, which could potentially cause brain damage and even death. While the chances of this are very low, it is better to be safe than sorry.

The decision to call your pediatrician can often be difficult, but trust your instincts about when your baby is ill. The best rule of thumb is to call your doctor if your baby runs a fever over 101°F. You know your baby better than anyone. A good pediatrician will understand your concerns and let you know if she thinks your baby requires an office visit.

How to Start with Solid Foods

The introduction of solid food into your baby's diet is an important milestone and can be fun. Watching your baby open her mouth and take food on a spoon makes her look like she is growing up!

To make this transition easier we suggest starting with one tablespoon of rice cereal mixed with four to five tablespoons of breast milk or formula. At first your baby will probably push the food back out with her tongue. This is normal.

Feed your baby one serving of rice cereal a day until she begins to master the concept of swallowing solid food. You should continue your normal schedule of breast or bottle feeding. Our babies each took a while to "learn" how to eat the cereal. After several days, if your baby is learning and eating well, then consider increasing the volume to two to three tablespoons of rice cereal three times a day and increase the consistency so that the cereal slowly gets thicker. It takes anywhere from two to eight weeks before your baby is successfully eating cereal three times a day. Be patient. Your baby will learn at her own pace.

After two weeks of eating cereal three times a day, you may introduce strained or mashed vegetables. Start with yellow or orange vegetables, such as squash, sweet potatoes, and carrots. Introduce only one vegetable every few days. This allows you to identify any vegetables that cause an allergic reaction. Next, you can add various green vegetables. We introduced vegetables in the following order: squash, carrots, sweet potatoes, peas, and then green beans. Once you have introduced all of the vegetables, fruits can be introduced. We recommend feeding vegetables for three weeks before introducing any fruits. The risk of introducing fruits first is that it could lead to a preference of fruits over vegetables.

If your child suffered from colic, you may want to delay introducing apples or fruit mixes that contain apples or apple juice. A recent study showed that babies who suffered from colic became very fussy when given apple juice.

Don't let *your* food preferences limit what you offer your baby. The more foods your baby is exposed to while she is young, the more foods she will like as she gets older.

Teach Your Child to Play Alone

With our first child we had to fight the temptation to be his sole source of entertainment. We know that it is so much fun to play with your baby, but you are doing him a disservice if you don't let him explore and play on his own some of the time. Playing alone can be a very enjoyable and enriching time for your baby.

When your baby is about three months of age, begin giving him playtime alone in a safe area. Lay him where there are interesting things to observe. You can stay nearby but you need to be out of sight so that you don't distract him. At first, your baby may only be able to spend a few minutes alone without crying out for your company. However, if you give your baby time to play alone daily, then your baby will increase the time he will be able to enjoy playing by himself to nearly thirty minutes.

The goal is not to ignore your baby; rather, it is to help your child learn to concentrate and be able to enjoy playing without a parent's involvement. We used this method with our children with great success. They now truly enjoy their play alone time. It is their time to play and do what they want without anyone interfering with their play.

Special Activities Are Fun for Everyone

While your baby is probably fairly happy with activities around the house, we suggest exposing her to fun outside activities. There are many options. Use your imagination. Here are some suggestions:

- *The Zoo.* Take your baby to the zoo. Many zoos have petting areas and special play areas for infants. Even in the winter months most zoos are open, and the inside exhibits are great for letting your baby watch the animals.

- *Story Time.* Story times are usually available at most public libraries. In addition, bookstores, such as Barnes & Noble and Borders, offer infant and toddler story time.

- *Science Museums.* Many science museums have wonderful infant play areas, which are safe and loaded with toys and objects that are sure to interest your little one.

- *Mall Play Areas.* While you may not love malls, the new play areas are nice. They offer the opportunity for your baby to interact with other children at no cost, and you can get other errands done on the same trip.

- *Pool.* Children as young as six months can enjoy the infant pool. In the winter, look into recreation centers that offer pool open hours.

- *The Park.* Even young babies can swing on your lap or in infant swings available at most local parks. In addition, being outside and watching other kids play will provide a lot of interesting activity for your baby. Bring a blanket and let your baby sit or lay back and watch all of the excitement.

- *Nature Areas.* When our children were about nine months old, we took them to a large field to watch us fly a kite. We discovered that they didn't care about the kite, but did love just being outdoors. Also check out nature reserves and trails. These are great places to stroll with you baby while taking in so much beauty.

Three Keys to Keeping Your Marriage Strong During Your Baby's First Year

Keeping your marriage strong during your baby's first year and beyond is an important ingredient for effective parenting. It is difficult to be a great parent and provide a healthy family environment if you and your partner don't have a solid relationship. The following three simple actions can be very helpful in maintaining a healthy relationship:

1. *Go to bed together.* Yes, this means at the same time and in the same bed! This provides an opportunity to talk and cuddle and helps keep you in sync with your partner.

2. *Have a date night every two weeks.* This time away together is critical for two reasons. First, it will help keep the romance and closeness alive that led you to marriage. Second, it provides a needed break from child-centered activities and helps increase your energy to handle the challenges of parenting. If you can't manage a babysitter that often, shoot for at least once a month.

3. *Dedicate at least fifteen minutes a day for "couple time."* This is time that you and your spouse reserve to catch up on each other's day, discuss concerns, etc. This can be after dinner, during a walk, or after your baby has gone to bed. What is most important is to have no distractions during this conversation time. Turn the television off and really listen and talk to your partner.

The first year with your baby will be busy, but remember that your relationship is a top priority and needs attention just as your baby does.

Introduce Toothbrush, Spoons, and Forks Early

We introduced the toothbrush to each of our babies once their first tooth emerged. Although not yet needed, introducing the toothbrush early promotes good dental health. In the beginning, we simply let our babies hold and chew on the toothbrush. Once more of their teeth came in, we started showing them how to brush their teeth.

We found that brushing our baby's teeth was a good activity to finish our bedtime ritual. Also, our babies were more enthusiastic about brushing their teeth when we brushed our teeth at the same time. By initially presenting the toothbrush in a positive way, we now find that our children get excited about "toothbrush time."

Similarly, introducing spoons and forks early can help your baby learn to feed himself at an earlier age. At five or six months of age give your baby an infant spoon to hold while he is waiting to eat or when he is playing. This will help him get used to holding a spoon or fork. Then, when it is time for him to learn to eat on his own, he will already be accustomed to holding a utensil. An added benefit is that baby spoons are great for biting on to help with teething pain.

Eliminate the Pacifier by Your Baby's First Birthday

I f your baby uses a pacifier, the best time to wean him from the pacifier is before he is a year old. This can be a difficult task because many children are hooked on their pacifier. It will be much easier to break the pacifier habit at ten, eleven, or twelve months than it will be when your baby is two years old and asserting his independence. When you make the transition, it is important that your baby have some other attachment object available, such as a special blanket, teddy bear, or toy that he really likes.

Research shows that use of a pacifier may increase the chance of several difficulties, including ear infections and dental problems. Long-term use of pacifiers is also associated with oral candidosis (thrush), respiratory and intestinal illnesses, tooth decay, and malocclusion (inappropriate alignment of teeth).

We took our oldest child's pacifier away when he was nine months old. See our section on "Breaking the Pacifier Habit" for tips. Out of sight was out of mind. He was a little out of sorts for a day or two, but it was much easier than we anticipated. Having his teddy bear available and giving him extra hugs and kisses during the transition was helpful.

Some of Our Favorite Baby Items

When we were expecting our first child we were astonished at how many things were needed to take care of one little baby. Everyone knows the basics: crib, stroller, car seat, playpen, and highchair. But, the following is a list of items that made our job as new parents easier.

- *Outdoor Blanket.* GoBlanket makes a great blanket for baby to sit on inside or out. This blanket is fleece on one side and a waterproof but breathable material on the other side. Made by eclogue (http://www.eclogue.com).

- *Bibs.* Plastic bibs by Burpee or Tommee Tippie were easy to clean and reuse. Tommee Tippie bibs are a little large so we found them more useful when our children were nine months old.

- *Nighttime Diapers.* Once your little one is sleeping through the night, we strongly recommend nighttime diapers to keep your baby dry during the night (this is especially necessary for boys). Regular diapers often can't handle a baby's nighttime volume. Try Huggies Overnight.

- *Diaper Genie.* One of your first purchases should be a Diaper Genie. This diaper disposal system keeps your house from smelling like one big dirty diaper. Once your baby starts eating solid foods, switch to the toddler refill. The plastic is thicker and great at keeping the smell of stinky diapers contained.

- *Spoons and forks.* Sassy spoons and forks are soft on gums, comfortable to hold, and indicate if the food you are serving is too hot. For on-the-go feeding, Boon makes an amazing feeding spoon called a Squirt. The bottom half of the spoon unscrews and holds several ounces of baby food. Once it is assembled, all you have to do is squeeze the baby food from the filled compartment to the spoon.

- *Mobile.* Sassy makes a colorful mobile that plays classical music and can be disassembled and used as a toy after your baby outgrows her mobile. We recommend buying a second different mobile to hang over your diaper-changing table.

- *Diaper Bag.* One Step Ahead makes an awesome diaper bag that is easy to keep organized and big enough for a day outing. It has insulated pockets and can hold at least four bottles or sippy cups. We also liked the Mother Ship Diaper Bag by Fluerville. It is easy to keep organized with lots of pockets and is available in many stylish colors and patterns. Finally, we recommend the Daiper Dude diaper bag for Dads. It has all the essentials, but still looks manly.

- *Bottles.* We liked both the Avent brand and Dr. Brown's bottles. We recommend you buy at least two days worth of bottles. It is worth the investment not to have to wash bottles everyday.

- *Dishwasher Container.* Invest the few dollars in a dishwasher baby-utensil holder. It is great at holding bottle nipples and other bottle parts, pacifiers, and sippy cup pieces. It is perfect at keeping them from melting on the heating element in the dishwasher.

- *Infant Car Seat Liner and Cover.* JJ Cole makes a great product called Bundle Me. It is a fleece liner that fits right into your baby car carrier. It keeps baby snug and warm in the winter and eliminates the need for blankets and coats. JJ Cole makes an identical product to fit your baby jogger or stroller too.

Avoid Sugar-Sweetened Foods

During their first year, babies try different tastes, textures, and colors in their food and develop their likes and dislikes. Most infants are willing to try almost any food during this time. Because of this, your baby's first year is the perfect time to introduce a variety of healthy and nutritious foods. Introducing healthy foods at an early age will go a long way in establishing a lifetime of healthy eating habits.

Some baby foods have added sugar that babies don't need. Sugar is considered a main factor in the huge increase in child and adult obesity. Added sugar can be hidden in the form of concentrated pineapple juice as an ingredient. Also, stay away from baby food labeled as "dessert." Babies in their first year of life don't need anything as sweet as these deserts. Your little one is much better off with an unsweetened fruit or unsweetened applesauce.

This is an important time for your baby as his lifelong food preferences are being formed. Research indicates that food preferences are usually formed in early childhood and then tend to persist. You can give your baby a big head start in healthy eating by avoiding foods that have added sugar.

Favorite Books for Reading with Your Baby

The number of children's books available is staggering. While it is wonderful that there are so many titles to choose from, it can be a little overwhelming, too. The following is our top ten list of books for baby's first year:

1. *Moo, Baa, La La La* (Sandra Boynton)

2. *Touch and Feel Series* (especially the animal-related ones)

3. *The Mitten* (a Ukrainian Folk Tale)

4. *Where's Spot?* (Eric Hill). The whole Spot series is great.

5. *Goodnight Moon* (Margaret Wise Brown)

6. *Guess How Much I Love You* (Sam McBratney)

7. *Skip to My Lou* (we like the one by Hoberman & West cott)

8. *My Many Colored Days* (Dr. Seuss)

9. *Very Hungry Caterpillar* (Eric Carle)

10. *Doggies* (Sandra Boynton)

We recommend buying the boardbook version of each book for use during the first year. Babies love to hold and chew on books. Boardbooks allow you to read to your baby without worrying that your baby will tear the pages.

Books were a big part of our babies' playtime. We stored our books on a floor level shelf in our playroom so they could easily grab a book without our help. Once our babies learned to crawl, it was one of the first places they went every day. They love to sit and play with the books, and we enjoy reading to them.

Ear Infections Are Tough to Diagnose

While many illnesses are fairly simple to diagnose, knowing when your baby has an ear infection is often a challenge. The signs of an ear infection are often subtle and can change depending on how severe and painful the ear infection is. Since ear infections typically occur after a cold, you should be on the lookout anytime your baby has a consistently runny nose for more than two weeks.

Typical signs of an ear infection include

• fever

• fussiness

• tugging at ears

• recent cold symptoms (runny nose, cough, etc.)

• shaking of the head

• unwillingness to suck on a pacifier

• waking up at night crying

Your baby may show only one or two of these symptoms or none at all. All of our children's ear infections occurred after they had a runny nose for one to two weeks. Even though their noses stopped running, they were fussier than usual and waking up at night crying. We were correct in diagnosing our babies' ear infections only about fifty percent of the time. However, even the times that we took our children to the doctor and found out that there wasn't an ear infection were helpful trips. Knowing the baby didn't have an infection helped us to look for other sources of distress, and made it easier to be firm at bedtime.

The only foolproof way to diagnose an ear infection is to have a pediatrician do a quick examination. Long term untreated ear infections can cause damage, so our rule is: When in doubt, get your baby checked out.

Eight Keys to Losing Postpartum Weight

O h, the joys of motherhood! You have this beautiful little person whom you created...and this bulging body. Trust us, you can and will get your body back. Here are our eight keys to getting there:

1. *Eat regularly.* Ensure that you are eating at least three meals every day. A large study shows that skipping meals actually reduced a new mother's weight loss. Many recent health books recommend eating five smaller meals a day (versus three larger ones), because the smaller ones increase the number of calories you burn each day.

2. *Exercise with your baby.* Studies show that women who exercise with their baby, usually by taking walks, lost more weight than those who exercised alone.

3. *Eat protein at every meal.* Proteins burn more energy and helps you feel full longer.

4. *Lift weights.* Use weights or do resistance exercise after four months post-partum. Resistance exercise increases metabolism and releases growth hormone, which is a key hormone for fat burning.

5. *Don't diet.* Skip the fad diets and concentrate on eating healthy meals instead. Over ninety-five percent of diets are unsuccessful, and most dieters end up regaining even more weight.

6. *Get your calcium.* Be sure to get at least 1200 mg of calcium every day. Studies show that it is very difficult to lose weight if your diet is low in calcium.

7. *Add iron if necessary.* If you are low on energy, get your iron level checked. Many women have an iron deficiency after childbirth. Often, a multivitamin alone does not supply enough iron to solve this problem.

8. *Be patient.* After the birth of our twins, I truly never thought I would get my figure back. I gained sixty pounds and had a complicated delivery that left me feeling exhausted. I gave myself one year to lose the weight. The first thee months I ate what I wanted and didn't worry about exercise. I took care of my babies and myself. After that, I slowly started walking more regularly and cutting out my nightly ice cream cone. Despite my lack of effort, by our twins' first birthday I had lost all but three pounds and could wear all of my old clothes. The moral of the story is that time does heal. Remember that your body has just been through a trying ordeal. Be patient. It will regain its shape slowly and at its own pace.

By following these steps you won't have the dramatic weight loss offered by many fad diets, but you will lose excess fat in a healthy and sustainable manner.

Good Sleep Equals a Happier Baby

For most adults getting adequate sleep seems simple. If you need more sleep, then you either go to bed earlier or sleep later. Unlike adults, babies need help in order to get the amount of sleep they need.

One of your jobs as a parent is to make sure your baby is getting sufficient sleep. If your baby is older than three months and is being consistently difficult or irritable, then she is probably not getting enough sleep.

There are two things that we found particularly surprising regarding our babies' sleep needs. First, our babies consistently needed to nap within two and a half hours after waking up in the morning. This was counterintuitive because they had their shortest time awake right after sleeping all night. We learned to accept rather than fight this tendency. Second, we found that when our children were being particularly difficult, it was a very strong sign that they were overly tired. When this occurred with some regularity, we would reexamine our schedule and adjust the schedule until we saw an improvement.

If You Walk or Jog, Buy a Baby Jogger—TODAY!

We strongly recommend a baby jogger. Even if you are not a runner, the baby jogger is very convenient for walks or short trips. If you are a jogger and want to run with your baby, these are a must-have. A trip in the jogger provides your baby with the opportunity to look at a variety of interesting things while also providing parents the opportunity to get some exercise and fresh air.

Other parents have told us they used their joggers until their children were four years old and beyond. The jogger can be used to take children to the pool and outdoor events. The oldest and most tried and true brand seems to be Baby Jogger, but there are several excellent models on the market. Baby Jogger makes single, double, and triple joggers. Their website is: (www.babyjogger. com). A recent newcomer to the baby jogger scene is the BOB stroller. Although more expensive that Baby Jogger, the BOB packs a lot into its jogger and gets great reviews.

We made it a weekend morning ritual to pack our babies up and take a walk each morning. While our children would normally become fussy towards the end of the morning, they behaved much better while on a walk in the jogger. They loved to point at dogs, cats, and other animals that we would often see on our walks.

Once your baby is six weeks old she should be able to sit safely in the jogger. Most brands of baby joggers can be outfitted with either sun canopies or wind and rain screens so that you can use them almost year round. We bought the rain and sun canopies for our jogger and found them very useful. The rain canopy was used on rainy days and on cold days when we wanted our babies to be extra warm. The clear rain cover creates almost a little green house where our babies could be snuggly warm and still take in the view.

During your baby's first few weeks of life he will tend to have a bowel movement between four and eight times per day. By the time your baby is four weeks old, he should producing about four stooled diapers a day. Some time around eight weeks of age, most babies will average one bowel movement per day. Formula fed babies will usually have more stooled diapers because there is more debris left over from the digestion of formula. Babies who are exclusively breastfed generally have looser stools and do not suffer from constipation. Once you introduce baby foods, the likelihood of constipation increases. When an infant is constipated, the longer the stool remains inside, the more moisture is removed by the intestines which makes the stool firmer and hard to pass. Long term it is best if you can keep your baby's digestive system running smoothly rather than having to try to fix a constipation problem frequently.

Your choice of foods will have an impact on your baby's stool. The following is a quick overview of the effects of some common baby foods:

- Foods that tend to create firmer stools: Applesauce and rice cereal.

- Food that may be constipating: Carrots and Squash.

- Foods that make stools softer: apricots, peaches, peas, pears, plums, and prunes.

If your baby's stools are too firm and he is having trouble passing them, there are a number of home remedies you can try. First, try offering prune juice twice a day. A warm bath will sometimes help to relax the muscles that may be holding the stool in place. If these steps don't help solve the problem, then it is a good idea to discuss the problem with your pediatrician. A good rule of thumb is that after two months of age if your baby if formula fed and doesn't poop for more than three consecutive days, you should contact your pediatrician. If your baby is breastfed and he goes more than six days without a bowel movement, you should contact your pediatrician. Other conditions that warrant an immediate doctor's visit are constipation accompanied by vomiting or blood in the stool.

Many pediatricians recommend a stool softening powder called Glycolax (or the over counter equivalent sold as MiraLax). One of our sons had continual difficulties with constipation. Using Glycolax was an amazing fix and it worked by just adding a small amount of the odorless and tasteless powder to water. As always, remember to check with your pediatrician before administering any medication to your baby.

If your baby is really having difficulty, a glycerin suppository dosed for infants and children can usually help solve even the worst constipation problems. Again, we recommend that you check with your pediatrician first. We had to use these suppositories a total of three times and each time they almost immediately resolved that episode of constipation. Once your baby is no longer constipated, start taking steps to prevent a reoccurrence by being aware of the foods that help and those that hinder easy digestion and elimination.

Immunizations Are Safe and Necessary

The furor about inoculations being dangerous is fortunately unfounded. If you search the Internet you may find questionable information regarding the alleged dangers of vaccinations. These concerns are typically overblown and sometimes completely inaccurate. Our best advice: Make sure your child gets the most current vaccinations as recommended by the American Academy of Pediatrics. At the back of this book we include a copy of the U.S. Center for Disease Control's recommendations for immunizations.

One vaccine that caused a lot of concern in the past was the oral polio vaccine that used a weakened live poliovirus to provide immunity. Unfortunately, in some cases the weakened virus actually caused polio. This method of vaccination is no longer recommended or used.

The polio vaccine now contains a dead virus that does not cause polio. The pertussin component of the old DTP vaccine—now called DTaP vaccine (diphtheria, tetanus, acellular pertussin)—has been improved to reduce complications.

A recent concern that received a lot of press was a possible relationship between the MMR vaccination and autism. Although many scientific studies have investigated this concern, all have failed to establish any relationship between the vaccination and autism.

However, if your baby has any of the following characteristics, then you should discuss vaccinations in detail with your pediatrician:

• A mild to severe illness

- A history of seizures
- A parent or sibling with seizures
- Any serious reaction to past vaccination(s)

Never Leave a Baby Alone While She is Elevated

This advice seems obvious, but we include it because it is so easy to become careless. We asked other parents about this topic and nearly every one had an occasion when their baby moved unexpectedly and fell from an elevated location.

When one of our twins was young and still not moving about much, we placed him on our bed for a nap. When we heard a thud and a cry a few minutes later, we feared the worst. Fortunately, our son was scared but unharmed. We were very surprised that he was able to move all the way to the edge of our king size bed, but we learned a valuable lesson that day.

Most changing tables now have security straps, which are handy if you need to look away for a second while changing your baby. Also, when your baby is in her crib, always keep the side rails up and secure.

The Six Best First Year Toys

With three children all under the age of one at the same time, we definitely had a need for toys that would interest our babies. At the same time we didn't want our house to look like a toy store! Based on the play testing of our babies and the advice of countless friends and family, we recommend the following as our favorite first year toys:

- Gymini by Tiny Love (From one to eight months)

- Lots of boardbooks to look at, bite, and chew on (three months and beyond)

- Jumper Seat (three months to twelve months)

- Fisher Price Classical Chorus Singing Stars Gym (one month and beyond)

- Evenflo MegaSaucer (four months to on year)

- Leap Frog Leap Start Learning Table (six months and beyond)

There are three other playthings that our babies used during much of their playtime. First, our kids loved playing with any kind of ball starting at about five months of age. Second, we were given a very large stuffed dog that our children loved to hug, climb on, and play with. Finally, a set of soft blocks that we used to build towers were a big hit starting at around six months of age. We guarantee your child will take great joy in knocking down a tower of blocks over and over again.

Ibuprofen Outperforms Acetaminophen

The two most commonly recommended pain relievers for children are acetaminophen and ibuprofen. Acetaminophen (brand name Tylenol) is typically the first recommendation of pediatricians due to a very slight advantage in its safety. However, in studies indicating a difference between the two pain relievers, acetaminophen was typically less effective in relieving fever and pain than ibuprofen (brand names Advil or Motrin). In addition, most studies suggest the effects of ibuprofen last two to four hours longer than acetaminophen.

Several times when our son was having teething pain we gave him Infant Tylenol. Unfortunately, acetaminophen didn't seem to make a noticeable difference. Eventually we used infant Advil instead and found it to be effective for relieving teething pain.

One caution is to be sure that you use the proper dosages for any pain reliever. There have been some recent press reports about overdosing with Infant Tylenol. These potentially dangerous overdoses occurred because parents administered the highly concentrated Infant Tylenol by mistakenly using the dosage instructions for Children's Tylenol. Infant pain relievers are much more concentrated than children's pain relievers.

We recommend always double checking the right dose for your baby before giving her any medicines. Many physicians recommend waiting until your baby is at least six months old before trying ibuprofen. As with use of any medication, be sure to check with your doctor first.

Turn Off Your Baby Monitor As Often As Possible

A baby monitor can be a great tool when you are out of ear-shot of your baby during nap or sleep times. However, we caution you to limit the amount of unnecessary time that you have your monitor turned on. Many parents leave their monitor on almost all the time, even if they are in the next room, so that they can hear their baby breathe or move about.

Although it is natural to worry about your baby, constantly listening to him with a baby monitor has two disadvantages. First, your baby will normally make noise and cry a little during a normal nap. Responding too quickly to your baby may not give him a chance to learn to quiet himself. In fact, you may end up disturbing his normal sleeping pattern. Second, by being on perpetual alert, your stress levels will be higher and you will not get the break from your baby that you need. So keep your monitor handy, but listen in only occasionally.

Get Hearing and Sight Checked Early

It is very important to be sure that your baby isn't having any hearing or sight problems. The first six months are a crucial time for the development of the optic nerve. This is because nerves and connections develop based on the stimulus the child receives. Problems with vision or hearing can delay your child's development. Further, if a problem with your baby's hearing or sight is not corrected, then he may never be able to develop correct vision or hearing.

The good news is that most pediatricians routinely screen sight and hearing at each baby visit during the first year of life. If you are unsure if your pediatrician is doing these checks, ask!

You should take any concerns you may have about your baby's hearing or sight seriously. There are many problems that can be easily corrected if the problem is detected early. Don't be overly concerned, but do promptly relate any concerns you have in these areas to your pediatrician.

See the World (or at Least Your Neighborhood) with Your Baby

Taking your baby out to public places at an early age will help her become comfortable in different environments. This greater comfort and familiarity will help her to behave better in public settings as she grows older. Many parents avoid public outings due to fears of germs or out of concerns that their baby will cry or misbehave. Healthy infants can safely be taken to public places when they are only one week old. We took our children out frequently and they now really look forward to our family outings. Our children generally behave well when they are out in public, and we credit this good behavior to the fact that we have taken them out frequently.

Once your baby is three months old, it is a good time to start short outings that can help teach her good behavior. Don't expect your baby to stay in one place too long without becoming fussy. We recommend first taking your baby to places that you can leave fairly quickly if she becomes fussy. As you take her out more frequently, your baby will behave well for longer periods of time.

Many children love joining their parents for grocery or other shopping trips where they can ride in a cart. However, few children under one can be expected to last more than thirty or forty-five minutes sitting at a restaurant. If you avoid public outings, your infant may be less comfortable and more likely to cry or fuss as he gets older. So get out and enjoy!

Night Waking Cures

Once your baby is sleeping through the night, a middle of the night wake up call from your baby can be challenging for even the most patient parent. A baby who is usually a solid sleeper will have times when she wakens and won't go back to sleep. The key to dealing with this situation is to know how to minimize the disruption to your sleep while making sure your baby is ok.

If your baby has been consistently sleeping through the night when she begins a pattern of night waking, it is important to try to determine the cause. Typical causes of night waking are: illness, teething pain, new skill development, and an inconsistent schedule. Consider each of these causes.

The first step is to investigate. Does your baby have a dirty diaper? Is her foot or arm stuck in the crib rails? Is she sick or teething? If your baby is ill or is suffering from teething pain and awakens crying, then by all means comfort her (and when appropriate, medicate her).

However, if your child is healthy and there is no apparent cause for her crying, then we recommend a restrained response. First, give your baby a little time to go back to sleep on her own. If it becomes clear she won't sleep or if she is screaming, then go into her room and comfort her briefly, but don't pick her up. Leave the room. If she continues to cry, return after five minutes. Again, comfort her briefly but don't pick her up. If she continues to cry, keep reassuring her every ten minutes until she gets to sleep.

While a natural response is to want to rock her to sleep or take her into your bed, this can easily backfire by creating a night waking pattern. The best way to avoid creating a night waking habit is to check on your baby and provide brief reassurance without making your visit so enjoyable that she will want a repeat performance every night.

Our oldest child had a number of night waking episodes. He also has a good set of lungs. Some nights we swore he was going to bring the house down. When he first awoke, we would wait to see if he would work it out himself and return to sleep. Many times he would go back to sleep after crying for a couple of minutes. If his crying lasted five minutes, we would go into his room to investigate. If his diaper was not soiled and there was no other apparent reason for his waking, we would rub his back, give him a little hug without getting him out of his crib, tell him we loved him and that it was time for sleep, and then we would leave. He would usually cry for another five minutes and then fall fast asleep.

Many times we knew it would be easier that one night to bring him into bed with us or rock him back to sleep. But we also knew that the next time would be harder if we did that. Our goal was always to teach him how to fall asleep on his own. We think we succeeded. You can too.

Six Keys for Encouraging Child Development

e offer the following six keys to encourage your baby's development:

1. *Be encouraging.* Let your baby explore new places, people, and things. Exposing your baby to new experiences and being excited with her as she learns new things will encourage growth.

2. *Be excited.* Celebrate when your baby learns new skills and abilities. Be excited by the quirks and differences in your baby that make her a unique individual.

3. *Communicate.* Talk to your baby regularly. Tell her what you are doing as you make a meal or fold the laundry. If she coos or babbles back, acknowledge her and let her know that she is being heard. Our pat response was always "Really! Tell me more!"

4. *Stay focused.* Help your baby practice new skills until she has mastered them. Support her when she works to use what she knows in new environments.

5. *Provide the Right Environment.* Provide an environment where your baby is safe, loved, and not subject to inappropriate disapproval.

6. *Demonstrate proper behavior.* Set limits and teach what is and is not correct. Help your baby understand the unwritten rules of behavior by modeling them in your everyday life.

How To Not Spoil Your Child
Part One—5 to 8 Months

I f you can't spoil your baby in the first six months, what happens after that? According to Dr. Burton White, director of the Harvard Preschool Project, "The origins of spoiling lie in the period from 5½ to 7½ months." It is at this age that your infant will be curious and want to have interesting things to do and look at but will become frustrated because she is not able to move around well on her own.

The key at this stage is to provide a variety of interesting activities for your baby while she is playing alone, and then attend to your child before she cries for attention.

Some activities that our babies enjoyed at this age were: using a baby jumper, playing on a floor gym, making noises with a floor music toy, playing with a selection of Tupperware, and standing while holding on to an activity table.

According to Dr. White,

> Make a special effort during the period from five and one-half to seven and one-half months to go to the baby before she cries for you to play with her. By doing so you will be helping her to prevent over-development of the intentional cry for company. The more you engage in that type of behavior, the less likely she will be to demand more and more of your attention each day.

Teach Your Baby Sign Language

As your infant grows older his ability to understand and think develops faster than his ability to speak. Most children begin speaking when they are between twelve and twenty-four months old. At about nine months of age, your baby should be able to start communicating by sign language. By teaching your baby some basic sign language words, you can make it easier to understand and meet your baby's needs. This will help make parenting easier and your baby less frustrated.

There are other benefits to teaching your child sign language. Studies show that babies who use sign language early also learn to speak more easily than babies who do not use sign language. Recent research also shows that signing babies score higher in intelligence tests, understand more words, have larger vocabularies, and engage in more sophisticated play.

The best way to introduce a new sign is to show the sign and say the word before doing the activity the sign stands for. For example, show your baby the sign for "eat" as you say the word "eat" before each bite you feed her. After using the sign for a few days it is helpful to shape and move your infant's hands after you make the sign. If you repeat the sign every time you do an action and reward your baby's attempts to make signs, then she will learn signs within a couple of months.

We taught each of our first four babies to sign, and plan on using it with our fifth child as well. When our babies were between eight and nine months old, we started teaching them sign language. Our oldest son and youngest daughter picked up signing easily, while our twins took a little longer. Be patient and remember that signing takes time, but is worth the wait. At one year of age, our babies could tell us that they wanted milk or water instead of just crying and pointing in the area of the kitchen. This reduced our frustration and made meeting their needs much easier.

We have found that signing comes in handy even when your kids get older. For instance, our twenty-month old son signed that he wanted milk and a banana during a time when one of us was talking on the telephone. We were able to have a telephone conversation while accommodating our son's silent request. Signing is also a great way to communicate across the playground ("no" or "gentle" or "all done") or to remind your little one of manners (say "thank you" or "please") when in public.

An excellent starter book for baby signing is, *Baby Signs* by Linda Acredolo, Ph.D., and Susan Goodwyn, Ph.D. Drs. Acredolo and Goodwyn have conducted research for over twenty years to investigate and document the advantages of teaching sign language to infants. Their website (http://www.babysigns. com) offers a great deal of information about the benefits of teaching sign language to infants. At the back of this book, we have included drawings of sixteen signs that should be a good start for you and your baby.

How to Introduce Foods to Your Finicky Eater

Once your baby becomes capable of eating, she will eat most baby foods with little hesitation. However, some babies are more finicky than others. Finickiness increases as you introduce more and varied solid foods. Fortunately, there is an effective method to help your baby learn to love new foods.

Based on recent research and our experience, the best way to introduce a new food that your baby doesn't seem to like is through repetition without pressure. For example, if your baby doesn't initially like peas, offer a bite of peas before any other food for at least ten days. Don't pressure your baby to eat the peas, simply offer them. It may surprise you, but by the tenth day most children will not only like peas, but may love them! An in depth study showed that this method was effective over eighty-five percent of the time.

We tried this with our little ones and found that it really does work. Three of our four babies would eat anything and everything put in front of them. However, our younger son was a picky eater. He didn't like many of the foods that our other babies enjoyed. To avoid serving different foods at every feeding, we simply kept putting the foods he seemed to shy away from in front of him at every meal. After about two weeks, he began eating foods he had refused in the past.

Let Your Baby Roam

At around seven months of age, the average baby will begin crawling. Babies at this age absolutely love to explore their surroundings. Watching our babies begin to crawl and walk was very fun, but also presented some new challenges. A key decision at this point for us was deciding how much of our home our babies would be allowed to play and explore.

Although it requires more work, we believe that it is better to allow your baby to roam and explore as much as possible. That being said, you will definitely want to establish some areas as "off limits," such as specific kitchen cabinets, the bathroom, stereo equipment, etc. We jointly decided on the areas where we did not want our children to be for either privacy or safety reasons. The rest our house was open for them to explore, under our supervision and guidance. If they roamed into an area that was off limits or touched things that we didn't want them to, we simply said "no, that's off limits." We repeated as necessary and then moved them to a different area if they didn't listen. Over time, each of our babies learned where they could go and what they could touch in our house.

We believe that this ability to roam was important to our babies' development. It helped them to learn that there are limits, but also gave them many interesting areas to explore. As our babies have gotten older, we have noticed that they now have little hesitation in exploring when we introduce them to new places.

Teething Pain Starts Early—and Lasts for Most of the First Year

When our first child started drooling, we thought that he might be teething. When he continued drooling and began showing signs of teething pain we were baffled since we couldn't see any teeth coming in. Many resources we consulted reported that teething pain should only last a couple of weeks. However, each of our children showed signs of intermittent teething pain over several months.

While there are different views on teething, our experiences most closely match Dr. Spock's observations. According to Dr. Spock,

> The average age for the eruption of the first tooth is seven months, and the average age when teething symptoms first begin—chewing on chewable objects, including hands and clothing, noticeable drooling, fretfulness—is three or four months. So, it takes about three months of teething before each group of teeth appears.

This explains why your baby may continue to show symptoms of teething even when a group of teeth has clearly emerged—the next group of teeth is starting to emerge.

For infants less than six months old, infant Tylenol along with a local pain reliever like Anbesol is helpful. Once your baby is over six months old, we recommend infant Motrin or Advil for pain relief. For something for baby to chew on, try a washcloth with a corner wetted and then placed in the freezer. We also offered frozen wheat bagels as a snack, which our babies liked both as food and as something they could use to soothe their teething pain.

Teach Her the Right Way from the Start

E ven though she may not look like it at times, your baby understands much more than you may think. Your baby's ability to speak greatly lags her ability to understand speech and nonverbal communication. Because of this understanding, your little one can understand instruction and learn to behave correctly earlier than you may think. While letting your six-month-old play with the remote control or telephone might seem harmless at the time, it will be difficult to take that same "toy" away when your baby gets a little older and is able to walk and climb to get your remote control.

By setting limits like this early, you will help your baby to better understand her world. In addition, your little one will be less likely to get upset because she can't play with something inappropriate when you are in someone else's house. It is much easier to teach the right behaviors from the start rather than trying to correct problems when your child is two or three years old.

Manners Matter

Teaching your baby good manners, particularly while eating, can start quite early. There is no doubt that when your baby starts to eat solid food, she will make a mess. However, that doesn't mean that you should accept bad behaviors when your baby is eating. If you teach your baby correctly from the start, then not only will your daily life be easier and cleaner, but you will save yourself the hassle of having to break bad habits when your baby gets older.

Unacceptable eating behaviors include: throwing food, spitting food out, blowing "raspberries," dropping food on the floor, and banging on her tray. One thing that can make these behaviors hard to correct is how irresistibly cute a baby can be while making a mess. There were many times we had to turn away from our babies so they wouldn't see us laughing at their antics.

By correcting your baby when she starts bad meal time behavior you will make feeding times much more enjoyable. Correct her by first saying "no" in a firm voice. If she continues the bad behavior, then stop the meal. Wait a few moments while telling your baby why she is not being fed (i.e. "no throwing food") and then try to feed her again. Don't use long explanations on why it is bad to throw food, etc. Simply saying no to the behavior is sufficient and more effective. Repeat as necessary and don't worry if you have to cut a feeding short after a couple of tries. Her behavior may be trying to tell you that she is finished eating.

Stopping the meal may seem harsh, but it is harmless and necessary. Don't worry that your little one won't get enough to eat if a meal ends a little early; she will make up for it at the next feeding. Also, don't expect perfection. There will be messy times at the table—it is just a fact of life. Your goal is to eliminate inappropriate behavior and teach your baby how to behave at the table.

Focus on the Present

Every parent knows how amazing—and challenging—parenting can be. During our first year with our little ones, most days were extremely rewarding. However, there were other days when parenting seemed very hard. So why does parenting seem easy one day and difficult on other days?

After considering this question, we reached the conclusion that the more we focused simply on taking care of our babies, the easier parenting seemed. Simply put, focusing on the task at hand made the job easier. We found that taking care of our children was harder if we were thinking about all of the things we needed or wanted to do (laundry, housework, bill paying, shopping, etc.). As all parents know, the care a baby needs doesn't always fit neatly into the busy life of an adult's schedule. While caring for your baby, you need to forget about all the errands you need to run and practice living in the present with your baby. Wait until nap time or after your baby is in bed for the night to pay the bills or write a letter. If you are accustomed to using a daily to-do list you may need to rename it "things I want to do if I get enough time" list. Try to remember each day that there are few things we can accomplish that are more important than providing our time and love to our children.

We have three suggestions to help reduce the number of daily chores and errands that need to done. First, outsource as many tasks as possible. Second, do some errands such as grocery shopping with your baby. Third, delay or eliminate any tasks that aren't really required. Our grass doesn't get mowed as often as it should, but that's ok—we are raising children, not a yard.

Don't Ask Your Baby to Perform

I t can be very exciting when your baby learns a new skill, such as crawling or clapping her hands. It is natural to want to her to demonstrate her new skill to others. However, we advocate that you fight the temptation to put your baby in a position where you expect her to perform. Urging your baby to showcase her new skill may reduce her love of learning new things. While it is very healthy to celebrate and congratulate your child as she develops new skills and abilities, don't expect her to perform on demand.

We do offer some exceptions to this general rule. For instance, once your child has learned how to wave hello or goodbye, it's a great idea to encourage her to communicate these simple greetings as a lesson in manners. But, don't be disappointed if your baby uses her new skills mostly at times that are more to her liking than yours.

Avoid Walkers for Your Baby

We strongly advocate avoiding baby walkers. Statistics tell us 30–40 percent of babies using a walker will sustain an injury. Estimates suggest that twenty-five thousand walker-related injuries (primarily head injuries) are treated in hospitals annually. Canada banned the sale of walkers back in 1989. Despite the high level of injury, over 1 million walkers are sold in the United States every year.

Parents cite two common reasons for usng a walker: 1) To keep baby busy, and 2) To help baby learn to walk. While a walker will help to keep a baby entertained, research shows that using a walker is more likely to delay an infant's motor development.

There are safer and better alternatives that will keep your baby happily entertained. Stationary play products such as Evenflo's MegaSaucer and a jumper seat hung in a door way are safe and fun for a baby. Our babies truly enjoyed both of these play stations and it gave us peace of mind knowing that they were safe while playing.

Your Baby's Baby Fat

With our nation's obsession with weight, many parents are also concerned with their baby's size. The average baby will triple his birth weight during the first year of life. Until he starts crawling, your baby will not burn through all of the fat and calories that he consumes. This is natural. Infants need excess fat and calories to continue to grow and mature. Fat helps a baby's nervous system develop and fuels very rapid growth during his first two years of life.

One of our sons was five pounds at birth and weighed over twenty pounds at eight months. His upper thighs seemed huge to us! But he was healthy and was in the fiftieth percentile for both weight and height. People would make comments about how "healthy" he was, but we knew he was exactly the way he was supposed to be. He thinned out amazingly quickly once he learned to crawl and walk.

Our advice is to feed your baby according to your pediatrician's advice and not to worry about your baby's weight during the first year. Studies show that infants eat exactly the amount of food they need. Just make sure that you aren't cajoling your baby to eat more food than he wants to eat. It may be natural to want your baby to finish the entire portion that you prepared for him, but this is not good for your baby. Pushing a baby to finish a serving or eat more may contribute to eating problems later in life.

Your pediatrician should be monitoring your baby's progress on height and weight charts. Unless she expresses a concern, there is very little chance that you need to be worried. Just provide nutritious foods for your baby and trust him to eat the amount of food his body needs.

Baby Books and Magazines Often Offer Conflicting Advice

One of the best pieces of advice we received while awaiting the arrival of our first baby was to limit the number of child care books we read. (We recommend our book, of course.) While this may sound strange, it actually makes good sense. Many of the experts disagree and give conflicting advice. If you read every book on parenting, we guarantee that you would be more confused about how to care for your baby. As an example, if you searched for "infant sleep" on Amazon.com, it would return a list of over thirty-seven thousand books!

We recommend choosing books that follow a philosophy that you and your spouse feel comfortable with. We followed this advice and read only a few books that were highly recommended by various friends. Now that we have five children, we have read many more books, but have found that "expert" opinions often vary considerably.

We do suggest that you buy one or two good reference manuals that will cover a wide variety of topics. The reference manuals that we have been the most impressed with are *What to Expect The First Year* and the *Mayo Clinic Complete Pregnancy and Baby's First Year*.

The moral of the story is: take with a grain of salt most advice from books, magazines, or helpful people. Find a couple of good resources and rely on your pediatrician.

Foods to Avoid in the First Year

uring the first year, there are a number of foods that your baby should not eat. Foods to avoid include:

- Cow's milk (including ice cream, yogurt, cheese, and any product that uses cow's milk)
- Peanuts and any products containing peanuts
- Eggs
- Honey
- Popcorn
- Hot dogs
- Shellfish
- Whole grapes

Introducing milk, peanuts, eggs, or shellfish too early increases the chance that your baby will become allergic to the food. The older a baby is when she first tries a new food, the less likely she is to develop an allergy. If food allergies run in your family or if you suspect your baby is sensitive to certain foods, then you may want to hold off on peanuts and eggs until she is at least two years old. Avoid feeding honey to your infant because honey has a risk of carrying the botulism bacteria.

Although they don't have allergic properties, we have added hot dogs, popcorn, and whole grapes to the list because they are a few of the worst choking hazards for babies under the age of one. Always remember to cut food into very small pieces before feeding anything to your baby.

Baby Will Walk When She Is Ready

We live in a competitive society, and it is natural for parents to want to compare their baby's development. Most parents remember exactly when their children started to walk (we are no different—two of ours walked at 15 months, one walked at 14 months, and one walked at 11 months). It is not uncommon to hear parents of little ones talking about this important milestone and when it occurred. While comparison may ease fears or provide a point of reference for a new parent, the only thing that comes from becoming overly concerned with when your baby walks or crawls is unnecessary worrying.

Infants develop motor skills at different rates. The normal age to start crawling varies between five and fourteen months of age, while the normal age to begin walking is from six to eighteen months. The good news is that according to numerous studies there is little or no relationship between when babies walk or crawl and their abilities later in life.

While there are developmental activities that may indicate a problem, neither crawling nor walking are good measures of how your child is doing. According to developmental psychologist Susan Berger, Ph.D., "I absolutely believe that gross motor skills are the least predictive of anything meaningful to a child's development and overall adaptation to life." So, our advice is to relax and enjoy playing with your baby. She will develop skills on her own schedule.

Don't Be Overprotective

F inding the right balance between constantly monitoring your baby and letting him explore his world can be challenging. Overprotective parents often hover over their babies. This can result in a child who is afraid to explore and resists playing alone. Setting the groundwork early will pay dividends when your baby becomes a toddler. Here are a couple of key tips:

- *Set limits for your child.* Even in his first year, your baby will want to touch, open, and play with things that should be off limits. While you do want to remove truly dangerous items from your baby's reach, it is also important to teach your baby that some areas, items, and activities are off limits.

- *Daily play-alone time is important.* Play-alone time will teach your child to be happy and play by himself without needing constant adult interaction. This is an important skill for your baby's development.

- *Don't always respond immediately.* While you always want to investigate when your child cries, there are times when it is better not to respond immediately. For instance, if your baby has a minor spill, wait to see if he gets over it on his own or if you can offer sympathy from a distance, instead of scooping him up and comforting him immediately.

Letting your child learn to be independent will pay dividends as he gets older. He will play nicely by himself and be unafraid to enjoy new play areas.

Just Say No to Juice

While you may think it sounds like a welcome change or an important milestone to introduce juice to your baby, we recommend you avoid juice during your baby's first year. Even though juices seem nutritious because they are wholly or partially made from fruits, most juices are much sweeter than the fruit your baby eats. Juices are typically as sweet as a soft drink and don't offer much more nutrition.

A recent study published in a pediatrics medical journal shows that children drinking more than five ounces of juice daily are more likely to suffer from childhood obesity. Further, according to Dr. Neal Kaufman, director of the Division of Academic Primary Care Pediatrics at Cedars-Sinai Medical Center in Los Angeles:

> Humans were not meant to drink their calories. Liquids like fruit juice, composed mostly of sugars, are brought rapidly in the body promoting obesity. Childhood obesity is in epidemic proportions, putting our children at risk for serious diseases, such as diabetes.

Instead of juice, give your baby water if she needs something to drink. In their first year, babies don't need much more liquid than what they will get by nursing or through formula. At around one year of age, you can introduce milk or water if your baby is thirsty.

Watch What You Say in Front of Baby

Parents often talk about their babies while their baby is within earshot. The assumption is that the baby can't understand what is being said. This can be a damaging assumption. Infants are very empathic and understand a great deal more than we may think. Their ability to talk or communicate with us is far more limited than their ability to understand us.

Babies develop an ability to read faces and body language as early as five months of life. According to many experts, babies can start trying to manipulate parental behavior when the baby is as young as six months old!

Before having a conversation with your spouse about how your nine month old was a terror that day, remember your baby probably understands at least a part of what is being said. It is better to have this kind of conversation when your child is asleep or out of earshot. We also recommend refraining from any labeling comments in front of your child, such as "he is a difficult baby."

This labeling can occur with other people too. We sometimes have strangers or friends make a comment about our child that we disagree with. We recommend responding in a friendly way, but one that tells your child you don't agree with labels for your child. For instance, when our children were at our local park, another mother pointed to one of our children and said, "he looks like the shy one". While we were not offended by this remark, we did not want our baby to think we agreed with this assessment. We simply said, "All of our children can be shy at times and outgoing at other times."

Ways to Comfort Your Baby When He Has a Cold

The average child will catch between 50 and 150 colds and viral infections before they are teenagers. In the first year alone, the average baby will get sick between three and ten times. For the simple aches, pains, and runny noses associated with the common cold, at six months or older try ibuprofen or acetaminophen. Check with your pediatrician before administering cold medicines or antihistamines. While these medications can sometimes be helpful for treating cold symptoms, they can be dangerous if administered in the wrong dosage. Don't worry if your baby's appetite is reduced or he is sleeping more often. These are normal when a baby is ill.

Do make sure your baby is taking in enough fluid in the form of breast milk or formula. Bulb syringes are great for clearing stuffy noses, and lotion on tissues keeps runny noses from becoming chapped. Also try applying petroleum jelly at night to the skin under and around the nostrils and upper lip to prevent redness and soreness.

Many doctors recommend using a mist humidifier and propping your baby's crib mattress. We found that neither of these suggestions offered our children much relief. If you find that your baby is wheezing or showing other signs that he may be having problems breathing, then call you doctor immediately.

Remember that the average cold lasts ten to fourteen days. If your baby shows signs of runny nose, fever, or cough past two weeks, call your doctor.

No TV Baby!

We are amazed by how early in life a baby can become mesmerized by a television. Once our children were about three months old, they started paying attention to the TV if it was on.

There are a number of reasons why conditioning your child to television at an early age is not a good idea. Many TV shows and commercials use cues to get an adult's interest. These cues include sex-related themes, such as those typically seen in beer commercials, as well as advertisements and shows that get our attention by alerting us to danger or showing violence. The constant flickering of light and flashing of changing images can quickly overstimulate any baby.

The American Academy of Pediatrics recommends that children under the age of two should not watch television. The AAP policy states,

> Pediatricians should urge parents to avoid television viewing for children under the age of two years. Although certain television programs may be promoted to this age group, research on early brain development shows that babies and toddlers have a critical need for direct interactions with parents and other significant caregivers (e.g., child care providers) for healthy brain growth and the development of appropriate social, emotional, and cognitive skills. Therefore, exposing such young children to television programs should be discouraged.

Our recommendation is simple: Keep the television off when your baby is around.

Give Yourself a Year to Lose Those Pregnancy Pounds

E very woman wants to get her pre-pregnancy figure back quickly after delivery. While initial weight loss usually comes pretty easily, a women's body is programmed to retain a higher level of fat for up to a year after giving birth. This tendency to retain extra fat is particularly true if you are breastfeeding.

At six months postpartum, most women weigh at least ten pounds more than before pregnancy. At one year postpartum, less than 25% of women will be back to their pre-pregnancy weight.

If you lose the weight you want, then great! But if you don't lose this weight, then don't beat yourself up over it. If you get back within a few pounds you have done pretty well. The extra weight will come off eventually by eating healthy foods and exercising moderately.

What about the fashion models who get their figures back in within a few months? To start with, they are very lean genetically. Add to these good genes a lot of hard work and a personal trainer and it is possible to get back in pre-pregnancy shape quickly. However, normal women shouldn't be hard on themselves for carrying a few extra pounds. Accept the beauty of what your body did and is still doing to make you a healthy mother.

Opinions Are Free—and Freely Given

L et's face it, everyone that has had a baby has an opinion on parenting. Many people don't mind sharing these opinions. Some parents get frustrated when close relatives or even complete strangers feel the need to share their opinions on parenting. Rather than get annoyed or confused, just ignore what you don't agree with and continue doing things the way that you want.

Even very young infants are perceptive and will pick up on a parent's uncertainties. The more confident and consistent you are, the safer your baby will feel and the better behaved he will be.

However, if something isn't working, then consider changing it. If you are having a problem, then ask your pediatrician or a parent whom you respect for advice. They may be able to provide advice or a resource that may be helpful. However, be careful whom you ask for advice. Much of the advice we received was wrong and would have been counterproductive had we followed it.

Don't Criticize Your Partner's Parenting

You want your spouse to be involved in your baby's life, but you want him or her to do it your way. Sometimes without thinking about it, new parents express dissatisfaction with their spouse's parenting when things aren't done exactly as they want them to be. If you want your spouse to be more involved in your baby's care, then you need to learn that he or she may do things a little differently. Unless your partner is doing something that is truly unsafe, it is best to let him or her care for the baby in his/her own way.

One mother expressed it this way: "My husband wouldn't burp our baby in the same position I used. I didn't think his position worked as well and he learned on his own after a while what worked best." Parenting isn't an exact science and no one wants to feel incompetent when they are caring for their own baby. So, if you do need to offer advice to your partner, then be gentle when doing so and bite your tongue on the minor issues.

Take Your Baby Outside

Life outside your home is fascinating to a baby. We were amazed by how much our babies enjoyed playing when they were sitting in our front or backyard instead of sitting inside the house. When playing inside, our children seemed to need more attention and toys to remain happy. However, outside they were often very content just sitting in the grass. Our babies really enjoyed sitting outside once they could sit up on their own, which was at around six months of age.

After discussing this with a number of other parents, we found this to be a nearly universal phenomenon. We also discovered that our babies preferred our front yard over our backyard because in the front yard they could watch people and cars go by. Of course, in most areas of the country you can't comfortably sit outside all year long, but take advantage of the weather when you can. If you live in a major city such as New York, the more time you can spend with your child in Central Park or a similar park the better. Just watching people in these parks will keep your child entertained.

Babies Learn by Observing

Babies learn from observing and acting on their environments. A major part of their environment is their parents. Not only do babies develop mannerisms and accents from observing their parents, but studies show that their temperaments are significantly affected by their primary caregivers.

To be a good role model, you should reduce or eliminate any bad habits that you don't want your child learning. This includes common habits such as nail biting or snacking throughout the day.

There are opportunities almost every day to teach your baby by example. Your baby will learn more from how you interact with other people than she will from being told how to play with other children. So, the next time you are driving with your baby and someone cuts in front of you, remember that your baby is watching and learning based on your response. This is a great opportunity to teach your child a calm response rather than anger or rage.

Breaking the Pacifier Habit

Babies have an inborn desire to suck. While feeding fulfills a big part of this desire, non-nutritive sucking is also important. Sucking is one of the primary ways that babies calm themselves. Pacifiers can help with this need. Unfortunately, the pacifier can easily become an attachment object that can be difficult for your baby to give up.

We recommend eliminating use of pacifiers when your baby is nine or ten months old. To help you and your baby break the pacifier habit, we offer the following step-by-step guide.

First, because most babies have a need for an attachment object, make sure that your baby has a stuffed toy or special blanket available to use as his new attachment object.

Second, explain to him that you are going to stop giving him a pacifier.

Third, begin limiting the amount of time that your baby is allowed to have a pacifier. If he is allowed to have it during naps or at night, start by eliminating its use at these times. This may lead to some additional crying at first, but should resolve itself within two or three days.

Finally, stop allowing him a pacifier at all. You may be surprised how easily he gets over not having his pacifier available.

Once you have eliminated his use of the pacifier, then it is important to search out each and every pacifier in your home or car and either throw them out or ensure that they are out of your baby's reach and sight. Nothing is more frustrating than having your baby weaned from his pacifier only to find him with a pacifier in his mouth that he found under the bed!

An Easy Way to Wean from the Bottle or Breast

Most pediatricians recommend weaning babies from a bottle at one year. For many parents, weaning a baby from their bottle is a dreaded task. Fortunately, by using our gradual method you will find that getting your baby to kick the bottle habit doesn't have to be a big battle.

An important preliminary step in weaning a baby from the bottle is to introduce a non-spill cup at about six months of age. This gives your baby six months to get accustomed to a cup before beginning to eliminate his bottles. If your baby is well past six months of age, don't fret. Introduce the sippy cup today and give your baby a few weeks to get the hang of using it. The first step in weaning your baby from the bottle is to eliminate the bottle at one of his feeding times. Pick the feeding your baby seems to need the least. For us, the easiest bottle to eliminate was the one given after lunch. Feed your baby lunch and give him a cup of milk with his meal. After a week, eliminate his dinnertime bottle. Again, add a cup of milk to his meal to replace the calories and liquids he used to get from his bottle. At this point, your baby should only be getting a bottle after breakfast and before bed.

After giving your baby a week to adjust to this new bottle schedule, it is time to eliminate the morning bottle. Once the morning bottle is gone you are in the homestretch and the last step is to eliminate the bedtime bottle. The quickest way is to simply withhold the bottle and offer a cup of milk in its place. If your baby is having a difficult time giving up his bedtime bottle, we recommend a more gradual method. Try slowly watering down your baby's bottle over the course of one week. For example, if you give your baby an 8-ounce bottle at bedtime, use three instead of four scoops of formula. Slowly decrease the amount of formula so that the bottle becomes more water and less formula. This makes the bottle less appealing. At the end of the week, take the bottle away. We found that our children were a little crankier at bedtime for a few days after they had given up their last bottle, but they quickly got over it. In each case of weaning, we somewhat dreaded our baby's reaction to dropping their bottle but we were pleased with how quickly our babies adjusted to this change.

If you are breastfeeding your baby, there is no right or wrong time to wean your baby from breastfeeding. You may find that it is easiest to take the lead from your baby. Some babies are ready to wean at eight months of age, while others are happy to nurse well into the second or even third year. The decision of when to wean your baby from breastfeeding is a personal one and the timing should be decided by what is right for you and your baby.

When you do decide the time is right to wean, the best way to do it is gradually. Your milk supply will decrease as you decease your feedings and your baby learns to rely on other foods and liquids for nutrition. As with bottle feedings, the best way to wean is by eliminating one feeding at a time. Pick the feeding that you think will be the easiest to eliminate. If your baby is under one year of age, you can substitute this feeding with a bottle. If he is one year or older, you can offer him a sippy cup of milk or water. Sometimes it helps if you have someone else offer this feeding. Out of sight may be out of mind. If your breasts feel full and uncomfortable, express a little bit of milk when you would normally be nursing, but don't express a whole feeding's worth of milk. The goal is to simply relieve some pressure and prevent engorgement.

As with weaning from the bottle, we recommend that you continue to eliminate one feeding each week until you are down to one breastfeeding a day. Usually, the last nursing session to go is the nighttime feeding. When ending this last feeding, try to change the routine. For example, if you always nurse your child in the rocker in his room before bed, try having a special story time in another room. Even this subtle change can help. Give your child extra hugs and kisses to make up for the time at the breast that he may be missing and talk to him about what is going on. Remember, he probably understands more than your realize.

Although you may feel some sadness as you end this special time, remember that a whole new amazing time is about to begin. You will still be in charge of feeding your child, just in a different way.

How Not to Spoil Your Child
Part Two—8 to 15 Months

At around eight months of age your baby enters a new and important developmental stage. How you handle typical challenges can either promote or prevent spoiling. The overall key is for your baby to be able to indulge his curiosity, while understanding that some behaviors are unacceptable. Here are some keys to preventing spoiling.

- Provide an environment rich in interesting activities and choices.

- Don't over-respond to falls and mishaps. Allow your baby to calm himself from minor accidents.

- Don't reinforce bad habits. Don't respond to whining and don't overreact or reward any other behaviors that you want to discourage.

- When changing diapers, don't allow your baby too much latitude to protest. Change his diaper efficiently, but firmly, if he protests. Use a toy or something he can hold to help distract his attention.

- Be extremely consistent with any limits that you have set. Rules must be consistent for an infant to understand and accept limits.

While there are no guarantees in life, these steps will definitely reduce the likelihood of creating a "spoiled child."

Think Long Term

We have found that if you think through the implications of simple infant care decisions, then you can often avoid a lot of trouble in the future. For instance, we talk about helping your baby to learn to go to sleep by herself. While this may seem like a small thing, it can have a big impact on your time and your child. There are many parents who dread their baby's bed time because these parents must spend hours reading them books, rocking them, and doing almost anything to get their child to sleep. These problems often continue until the child is three or four years old. The key lesson to learn is that what often seems like the "easy" way to go may backfire in the long term.

One of the biggest areas to be aware of as your baby approaches one year of age is the effect of responding to whining and tantrums. Whining is often difficult to ignore. We didn't understand why until Yvonne Gufstason, Ph.D., a parenting consultant, explained, "A baby's whining tone is often identical to the pitch and tone a baby would use to signal real distress. So, the reason the whine is so effective at getting a parent's attention is that we (parents) are biologically programmed to respond." While giving in to a baby who is whining or is having a tantrum is the easiest way to end the episode, the long-term consequence is that your baby will whine or have tantrums more often.

Another example is allowing your child to walk instead of riding in the stroller (with the parent pushing an empty stroller while trying to keep the child moving forward). While it seems like a good idea because it is a chance for your baby to get exercise, and he may enjoy it for the short term, the downside is that your child may begin to protest any ride in the stroller or baby jogger. If you are going to have only one child, then this may not be a problem. However, if you have two or more young children, then it can become almost impossible to make it to your destination. A couple we know always drives their two children to the park, even though the park is only about six blocks away from their home. When we asked why they didn't walk, they told us, "They (their babies) can't walk that far yet, but they also won't ride in the stroller, so taking our car is the only way to get them to the park without having to carry them part of the way."

Our advice is to think about the future impact of your decisions. If you realize you've made a mistake, don't fret. Just be quick to change things that you find aren't working for your family.

Appendix A

First Year Schedules

1 Month of Age

TIME	ACTIVITY
7:00	Wake Up Feeding
7:30	Awake Time
8:00	Nap
8:30	
9:00	
9:30	
10:00	Feeding
10:30	Awake Time
11:00	Nap
11:30	
12:00	
12:30	
1:00	Feeding
1:30	Awake Time
2:00	Nap
2:30	
3:00	
3:30	
4:00	Feeding
4:30	Awake Time
5:00	Nap
5:30	
6:00	
6:30	
7:00	Feeding
7:30	Awake Time
8:00	Nap
8:30	
9:00	
9:30	
10:00	Feeding and then Back to Bed
10:30	Sleep
11:00	

At night, put your baby to bed and let her sleep until she awakens on her own. Feed as necessary through the night. Regardless of nighttime feeding times, be sure to wake your baby and feed her for your set start time of day (here 7:00 A.M.). This will help your baby to establish a consistent schedule.

2 Months of Age

TIME	ACTIVITY
7:00	Wake Up Feeding
7:30	Awake Play Time
8:00	
8:30	Nap
9:00	
9:30	
10:00	Feeding
10:30	Awake Play Time
11:00	
11:30	Nap
12:00	
12:30	
1:00	Feeding
1:30	Awake Play Time
2:00	
2:30	Nap
3:00	
3:30	
4:00	Feeding
4:30	Awake Play Time
5:00	
5:30	Nap
6:00	
6:30	
7:00	Feeding
7:30	Awake Play Time
8:00	
8:30	Nap
9:00	
9:30	
10:00	Feeding and then Back to Bed
10:30	Sleep
11:00	

At night, put your baby to bed and let her sleep until she awakens on her own. Feed as necessary through the night. Regardless of nighttime feeding times, be sure to wake your baby and feed her for your set start time of day (here 7:00 A.M.). This will help your baby to establish a consistent schedule.

3 Months of Age

TIME	ACTIVITY
7:00	Wake Up Feeding
7:30	Awake Play Time
8:00	
8:30	
9:00	Nap
9:30	
10:00	
10:30	Feeding
11:00	Awake Play Time
11:30	
12:00	
12:30	Nap
1:00	
1:30	
2:00	Feeding
2:30	Awake Play Time
3:00	
3:30	
4:00	Nap
4:30	
5:00	
5:30	Feeding
6:00	Awake Play Time
6:30	
7:00	
7:30	Nap
8:00	
8:30	
9:00	Feeding and then Back to Bed
9:30	Sleep for the Night
10:00	
10:30	
11:00	

At this point, your baby should be sleeping through to morning after her last feeding. If she is not, then let her sleep until she awakens on her own. Before responding, wait to see if she cries for a few minutes and goes back to sleep. If not, then feed her and put her back to bed. Be sure to wake your baby and feed her for your set start time of day (here 7:00 A.M.). This will keep her on a consistent schedule.

6 Months of Age

TIME	ACTIVITY
7:00	Wake Up Feeding
7:30	Play Time
8:00	
8:30	
9:00	Nap
9:30	
10:00	
10:30	
11:00	Feeding
11:30	Play Time
12:00	
12:30	
1:00	Nap
1:30	
2:00	
2:30	
3:00	Feeding
3:30	Play Time
4:00	
4:30	
5:00	Nap
5:30	
6:00	
6:30	
7:00	Bedtime Feeding
7:30	Sleep for the Night
8:00	
8:30	
9:00	
9:30	
10:00	
10:30	
11:00	

At six months of age, feedings generally include cereal plus nursing or a bottle. Omit the cereal at the last feeding of the day and simply nurse your baby or feed him a bottle and put him back to bed. Be sure to wake your baby and feed him for your set start time of day (here 7:00 A.M.). This will keep him on a consistent schedule.

9 Months of Age

TIME	ACTIVITY
7:00	Wake Up Feeding
7:30	Play Time
8:00	
8:30	
9:00	Nap
9:30	
10:00	
10:30	
11:00	Feeding
11:30	Play Time
12:00	
12:30	
1:00	Nap
1:30	
2:00	
2:30	
3:00	Feeding
3:30	Play Time
4:00	
4:30	
5:00	Nap
5:30	
6:00	Awake and Brief Playtime
6:30	Bath and Bedtime Feeding
7:00	Sleep for the Night
7:30	
8:00	
8:30	
9:00	
9:30	
10:00	
10:30	
11:00	

At nine months of age, feedings generally include jarred baby food, finger food, or cereal plus nursing or a bottle. Omit the solid or cereal at the last feeding of the day and simply nurse your baby or feed him a bottle and put him back to bed. Be sure to wake your baby and feed him for your set start time of day (here 7:00 A.M.). This will keep him on a consistent schedule.

12 Months of Age

TIME	ACTIVITY
7:00	Wake Up Feeding
7:30	Play Time
8:00	
8:30	
9:00	
9:30	Morning Nap
10:00	
10:30	
11:00	
11:30	Play Time
12:00	Lunch
12:30	
1:00	
1:30	
2:00	Snack
2:30	Afternoon Nap
3:00	
3:30	
4:00	
4:30	Playtime
5:00	
5:30	Dinner
6:00	
6:30	Bath and Bedtime Feeding or Snack
7:00	Sleep for the Night
7:30	
8:00	
8:30	
9:00	
9:30	
10:00	
10:30	
11:00	

At one year of age, you should begin weaning your baby from the bottle. Until he is totally weaned, offer him a bottle or breast feed at the bedtime feeding. Once your baby is weaned, you can offer a cup of milk and/or a snack before bed if desired.

Appendix B

Guide for Babysitters

A GUIDE TO ME

Angel Baby

Some babies really do come with an instruction manual

Family Information

Address: 1234 Main Street
   City, State 12345

Telephone No.: (555) 555-1234

Parents: Mommy and Daddy

Child: Angel Baby

Emergency Contact Information

Emergency: CALL 911

Dr. Pediatrician: 555-1212
(Central Pediatrics)

Mom:
Office Phone: (555) 555-5151
Cell Phone: (555) 555-2246

Dad:
Office Phone: (555) 555-4613
Direct at Work: (555) 555-5881
Cell Phone: (555) 555-2246

Grandma & Grandpa:
Work Number: (555) 555-2500
Home Number: (555) 555-5337

Nanny:
Anna Sweet   (555) 555-9605

Neighbors:
Jane & Mark   (555) 555-3282
Carol & Frank (next door) (555) 555-9922
Robin & Dan   (555) 555-4689

Other People Who Might Be Able to Help in an Emergency:
Julie Wonderful   (555) 555-6638
Ann Helpful   (555) 555-9110

Angel Baby Information

Date of Birth January 7, 2011
Height 25"
Weight 17 lbs
Drug Allergies None
Medications None

Loves: Learning new things and playing with her toys.

Dislikes: Not a lot, but when she is unhappy, she will let you know (WOW she can be loud!). She doesn't like to wait for her food or her bottle, so have it ready to go when it is time to eat. She is also teething right now. Feel free to give her ¾-teaspoon (3.5 ccs) of children's strength ibuprofen every 6-8 hours as needed for pain.

Miscellaneous: Angel Baby is crawling and loves to climb. (She is actually trying to master the stairs, so keep a close eye on her.)

Breakfast

- Angel Baby usually awakens and is ready to eat between 6:30 and 7:00 A.M.
- Play with her upstairs or down until 7:00 (we try hold breakfast until 7:00).

Food: Feed Angel Baby the following for breakfast:

- If Angel Baby is very hungry and inpatient while you prepare breakfast, give her a few Cheerios on her tray
- Any of her Gerber cereals (rice, oatmeal or mixed) mixed with a little baby fruit from the jar and water (the consistency should be thick).
- Finish with a bottle (usually 6 ounces). Use one scoop of formula for every two ounces of water.

AFTER BREAKFAST:

After breakfast, you can let the Angel baby play in the kitchen while you clean up. After clean up, get Angel Baby dressed for the day.

Lunch

- Angel Baby eats lunch at 11:30.

Food: Angel Baby is making the transition to table food.

1. Start with one or more of following steamed and finely diced vegetables

- carrots	- green beans
- corn	- zucchini
- squash	- sweet potato
- peas	

2. Main course

- ravioli (Gerber Graduates)	- turkey meat sticks (Gerber
- macaroni and cheese	Graduates)
- pasta cut into small pieces	
- Chunky Soup – after you heat it up, pour the liquid out and serve the solid parts	

3. Fruit—cut up into small pieces

- cut grapes	- mandarin oranges
- banana (sliced)	- pear (sliced or canned and cut into small pieces)
- peaches (canned and cut)	
- mango	- nectarines
- apple	- melon

4. Bottle—Finish by feeding Angle Baby her bottle. Make a 6-ounce bottle.

AFTER LUNCH:

After lunch, clean Angel Baby and take her upstairs. Change her diaper and put her down for her nap.

Dinner

- Angel Baby usually eats dinner when she gets up from her nap or shortly thereafter. Her menu is pretty much the same as lunch.

1. Start with one or more of following steamed and finely diced vegetables

- carrots
- corn
- squash
- peas

- green beans
- zucchini
- sweet potato

2. Main course

- ravioli (Gerber Graduates)
- macaroni and cheese
- pasta cut into small pieces
- Chunky Soup—after you heat it up, pour the liquid out and serve the solid parts

- turkey meat sticks (Gerber Graduates)

3. Fruit—cut up into small pieces

- cut grapes
- banana (sliced)
- peaches (canned and cut)
- mango
- apple

- mandarin oranges
- pear (sliced or canned and cut into small pieces)
- nectarines
- melon

4. Bottle—Finish by feeding Angel Baby her bottle. Make a 6-ounce bottle.

Bedtime

Baths

- Start bath time at about 6:15 P.M. so you can have Angel Baby in bed by 7:00 P.M.
- Bath Angel baby in the bath tub on the second floor.
- The bath stuff (toys, shampoo, and soap) is in the cupboard outside of the bathroom.
- Towel Angel Baby off and then get her dressed in the nursery next door to the bathroom.

Bedtime Bottle

- Angel baby gets an 8-ounce bottle at bedtime.
- She usually takes her bedtime feeding in the rocker in the nursery.

Bedtime routine

- Angel Baby likes to have music playing as she goes to sleep.
- We have a musical aquarium for you to turn on when you put Angel Baby to bed.
- She may babble and coo for a while after you leave, but she will go to sleep.
- Angel Baby just recently started crying out about 5-10 minutes after she goes down. She's been going through some separation anxiety and we think she just needs to know that we are there. Go in quickly, give her a hug and kiss and tell her it is bedtime and that you are just downstairs. She usually goes right to sleep without another peep.

Miscellaneous

- **Supplies**
- Supplies are in the nursery on the second floor (either under the diaper changer or in the cupboard) and also in the closet next to the diaper changer in the playroom.
- Extra formula is in the cabinet next to the pantry.
- Food is in the pantry cupboard and canned fruits and vegetables are in the cabinet next to the pantry.

- **Medication**—Ibuprofen for teething is fine. Dosage is 3/4 teaspoon (3.5 ccs) of children's strength every 6-8 hours.

- **Mixing Formula** – 1 scoop for every 2 ounces of water. So, for a 6-ounce bottle, use 3 scoops; for an 8-ounce bottle, use 4 scoops.

- **Taboo Foods**—No honey, peanuts, juice, sugar, cookies, hot dogs, popcorn, or other yummy food yet!

- **Security and Keys**—One key works for all the locks in our house (including the gates, garage, and storage shed). Lock up at night and turn the front porch light on.

- **Temperature Control**—The thermostat is set to run automatically (warmer during the day and cooler at night). If you want to change the temp, just push the up and down buttons and then push 'hold temp.' To restart program, push 'run program.'

- **Activities**
  1. **Walks.** Walks are wonderful if Angel Baby is getting antsy and it is warm enough. Make sure she is belted into the jogger. Her coat is in the front closet and her hat and mittens are in the basket by the side door.
  2. **Music.** Angel Baby loves music. There is a stereo in the armoire in the playroom.

- **Baby Safety**
  1. **Blinds.** Keep her crib pulled away from the blinds in her room and the blind cords up high so she cannot reach them.
  2. **Gates.** Keep the gates closed.
  3. **Bathroom Doors.** Keep these closed at all times.
  4. **Laundry Room Door.** Keep closed.

Appendix C

First Signs

MORE

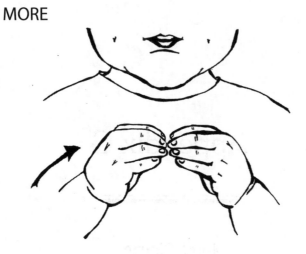

Tap fingertips together.

MILK

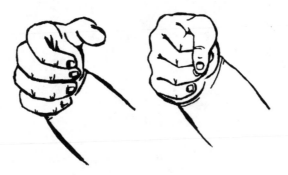

Open and close your fist as if milking a cow or pumping your hand.

WATER

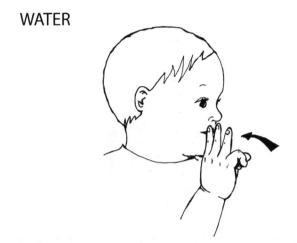

The sign for "water" is made by forming your right hand into the letter "w" with your fingers. Touch your mouth with your index finger. Repeat a few times.

FINISHED or
ALL DONE

Place both of your open hands in front of you. Each hand should face you, with your fingers pointing upward. Shake both hands quickly a few times with an outward motion.

PLEASE

The sign for "please" is made by placing your flat right hand over the center of your chest. Move your hand in a clockwise motion a few times.

THANK YOU
and GOOD

Touch your lips with the front of the fingers of your right hand. Your hand should be a flat palm. Move your hand away from your face, palms upward. The same sign is used for both "thank you" and "good."

STOP

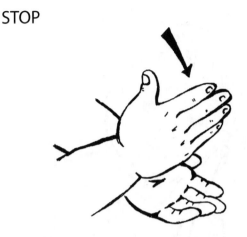

Extend your left hand, palm upward. Sharply bring your open right hand down to your left hand at a right angle.

HELP

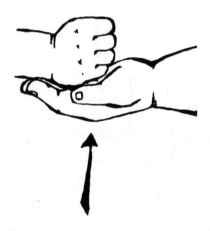

The sign for "help" is made by first closing your right hand. Place your right hand on the outstretched palm of your left hand. Raise both hands.

BED or SLEEP

Place both hands together and then place them to the side of your slightly tilted head.

DOG

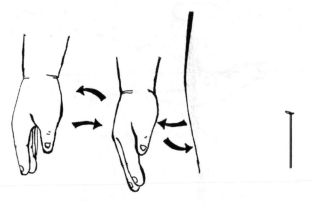

The sign for "dog" is made by slapping your right flat hand against your right leg, then snapping your fingers. This is a very flexible sign. You can snap your fingers, then slap your leg. You can slap your leg twice and not snap your fingers at all.

CAT

*Use your hand to pretend that you are pulling on imaginary whiskers.
You can use one hand or two.*

HOT

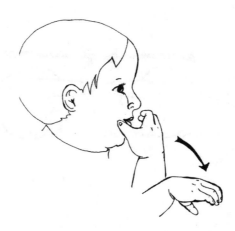

*Make the sign for "hot" by forming the letter "c" with your right hand.
Place your thumb and fingers at the sides of your mouth. Quickly turn
your hand forward to the right.*

COLD

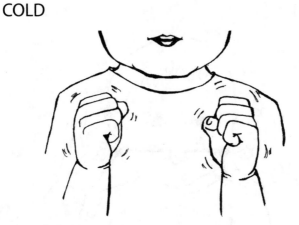

Make the sign for "cold" by forming both hands into fists. Hold both hands in front of you and shake them.

HURT or
PAIN

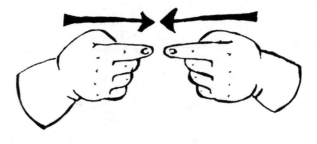

Extend the index fingers of both hands. Bring the fingers toward each other twice using a jabbing movement.

SORRY

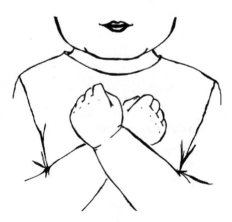

The sign for "sorry" is made by forming a fist with your right hand. Rotate your hand over your heart in a few circular clockwise motions.

LOVE

Cross both hands over your heart.

Appendix D

Growth and Height Charts

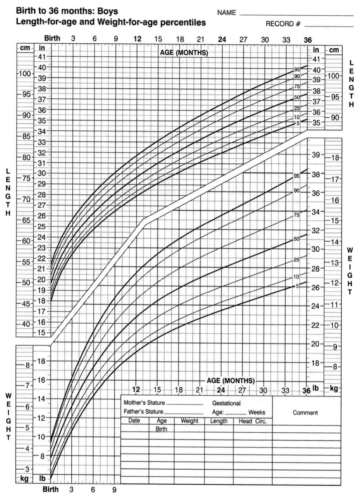

Birth to 36 months: Boys
Length-for-age and Weight-for-age percentiles

NAME _____

RECORD # _____

Available at **http://www.nal.usda.gov/wicworks**

SOURCE: Developed by the National Center for Health Statistics in collaboration with
   the National Center for Chronic Disease Prevention and Health Promotion (2002).
   http://www.cdc.gov/growthcharts

SAFER · HEALTHIER · PEOPLE™

Birth to 36 months: Girls
Length-for-age and Weight-for-age percentiles

NAME _____

RECORD # _____

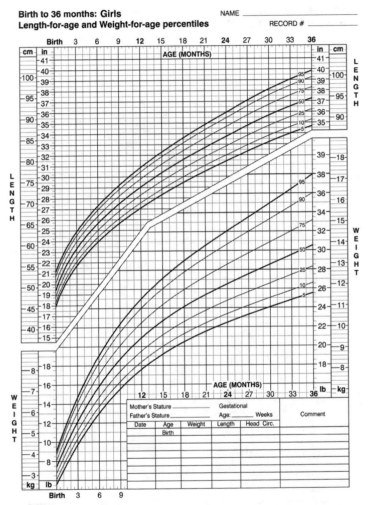

Available at http://www.nal.usda.gov/wicworks

SOURCE: Developed by the National Center for Health Statistics in collaboration with
the National Center for Chronic Disease Prevention and Health Promotion (2002).
http://www.cdc.gov/growthcharts

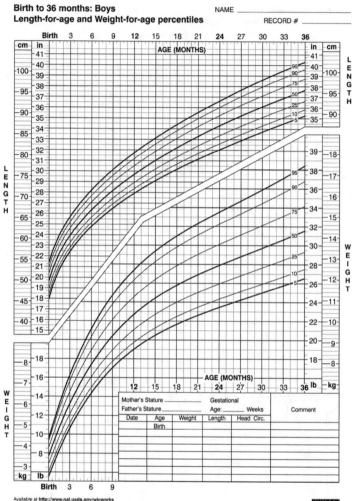

Birth to 36 months: Boys
Length-for-age and Weight-for-age percentiles

NAME _____

RECORD # _____

Available at **http://www.nal.usda.gov/wicworks**

SOURCE: Developed by the National Center for Health Statistics in collaboration with
the National Center for Chronic Disease Prevention and Health Promotion (2002).
http://www.cdc.gov/growthcharts

CDC

SAFER·HEALTHIER·PEOPLE™

Birth to 36 months: Girls
Length-for-age and Weight-for-age percentiles

NAME _____

RECORD # _____

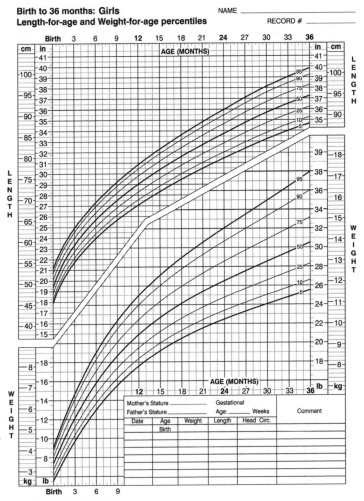

Available at http://www.nal.usda.gov/wicworks

SOURCE: Developed by the National Center for Health Statistics in collaboration with
the National Center for Chronic Disease Prevention and Health Promotion (2002).
http://www.cdc.gov/growthcharts

Appendix E

American Academy of Pediatrics
Immunization Schedule

Recommended Immunization Schedule for Persons Aged 0 Through 6 Years—United States • 2011

For those who fall behind or start late, see the catch-up schedule

Vaccine ▼ Age ►	Birth	1 month	2 months	4 months	6 months	12 months	15 months	18 months	19–23 months	2–3 years	4–6 years	
Hepatitis B[1]	HepB	HepB			HepB							
Rotavirus[2]			RV	RV	RV[2]							
Diphtheria, Tetanus, Pertussis[3]			DTaP	DTaP	DTaP	see footnote[3]	DTaP				DTaP	
Haemophilus influenzae type b[4]			Hib	Hib	Hib[4]	Hib						
Pneumococcal[5]			PCV	PCV	PCV	PCV				PPSV		
Inactivated Poliovirus[6]			IPV	IPV		IPV					IPV	
Influenza[7]						Influenza (Yearly)						
Measles, Mumps, Rubella[8]						MMR		see footnote[8]			MMR	
Varicella[9]						Varicella		see footnote[9]			Varicella	
Hepatitis A[10]						HepA (2 doses)				HepA Series		
Meningococcal[11]										MCV4		

Range of recommended ages for all children

Range of recommended ages for certain high-risk groups

This schedule includes recommendations in effect as of December 21, 2010. Any dose not administered at the recommended age should be administered at a subsequent visit, when indicated and feasible. The use of a combination vaccine generally is preferred over separate injections of its equivalent component vaccines. Considerations should include provider assessment, patient preference, and the potential for adverse events. Providers should consult the relevant Advisory Committee on Immunization Practices statement for detailed recommendations: http://www.cdc.gov/vaccines/pubs/acip-list.htm. Clinically significant adverse events that follow immunization should be reported to the Vaccine Adverse Event Reporting System (VAERS) at http://www.vaers.hhs.gov or by telephone, 800-822-7967.

1. **Hepatitis B vaccine (HepB).** (Minimum age: birth)
 At birth:
 • Administer monovalent HepB to all newborns before hospital discharge.
 • If mother is hepatitis B surface antigen (HBsAg)-positive, administer HepB and 0.5 mL of hepatitis B immune globulin (HBIG) within 12 hours of birth.
 • If mother's HBsAg status is unknown, administer HepB within 12 hours of birth. Determine mother's HBsAg status as soon as possible and, if HBsAg-positive, administer HBIG (no later than age 1 week).
 Doses following the birth dose:
 • The second dose should be administered at age 1 or 2 months. Monovalent HepB should be used for doses administered before age 6 weeks.
 • Infants born to HBsAg-positive mothers should be tested for HBsAg and antibody to HBsAg 1 to 2 months after completion of at least 3 doses of the HepB series, at age 9 through 18 months (generally at the next well-child visit).
 • Administration of 4 doses of HepB to infants is permissible when a combination vaccine containing HepB is administered after the birth dose.
 • Infants who did not receive a birth dose should receive 3 doses of HepB on a schedule of 0, 1, and 6 months.
 • The final (3rd or 4th) dose in the HepB series should be administered no earlier than age 24 weeks.
2. **Rotavirus vaccine (RV).** (Minimum age: 6 weeks)
 • Administer the first dose at age 6 through 14 weeks (maximum age: 14 weeks 6 days). Vaccination should not be initiated for infants aged 15 weeks 0 days or older.
 • The maximum age for the final dose in the series is 8 months 0 days
 • If Rotarix is administered at ages 2 and 4 months, a dose at 6 months is not indicated.
3. **Diphtheria and tetanus toxoids and acellular pertussis vaccine (DTaP).** (Minimum age: 6 weeks)
 • The fourth dose may be administered as early as age 12 months, provided at least 6 months have elapsed since the third dose.
4. **Haemophilus influenzae type b conjugate vaccine (Hib).** (Minimum age: 6 weeks)
 • If PRP-OMP (PedvaxHIB or Comvax [HepB-Hib]) is administered at ages 2 and 4 months, a dose at age 6 months is not indicated.
 • Hiberix should not be used for doses at ages 2, 4, or 6 months for the primary series but can be used as the final dose in children aged 12 months through 4 years.
5. **Pneumococcal vaccine.** (Minimum age: 6 weeks for pneumococcal conjugate vaccine [PCV]; 2 years for pneumococcal polysaccharide vaccine [PPSV])
 • PCV is recommended for all children younger than 5 years. Administer 1 dose of PCV to all healthy children aged 24 through 59 months who are not completely vaccinated for their age.
 • A PCV series begun with 7-valent PCV (PCV7) should be completed with 13-valent PCV (PCV13).
 • A single supplemental dose of PCV13 is recommended for all children aged 14 through 59 months who have received an age-appropriate series of PCV7.
 • A single supplemental dose of PCV13 is recommended for all children aged 60 through 71 months with underlying medical conditions who have received an age-appropriate series of PCV7.

 • The supplemental dose of PCV13 should be administered at least 8 weeks after the previous dose of PCV7. See MMWR 2010:59(No. RR-11).
 • Administer PPSV at least 8 weeks after last dose of PCV to children aged 2 years or older with certain underlying medical conditions, including a cochlear implant.
6. **Inactivated poliovirus vaccine (IPV).** (Minimum age: 6 weeks)
 • If 4 or more doses are administered prior to age 4 years an additional dose should be administered at age 4 through 6 years.
 • The final dose in the series should be administered on or after the fourth birthday and at least 6 months following the previous dose.
7. **Influenza vaccine (seasonal).** (Minimum age: 6 months for trivalent inactivated influenza vaccine [TIV]; 2 years for live, attenuated influenza vaccine [LAIV])
 • For healthy children aged 2 years and older (i.e., those who do not have underlying medical conditions that predispose them to influenza complications), either LAIV or TIV may be used, except LAIV should not be given to children aged 2 through 4 years who have had wheezing in the past 12 months.
 • Administer 2 doses (separated by at least 4 weeks) to children aged 6 months through 8 years who are receiving seasonal influenza vaccine for the first time or who were vaccinated for the first time during the previous influenza season but only received 1 dose.
 • Children aged 6 months through 8 years who received no doses of monovalent 2009 H1N1 vaccine should receive 2 doses of 2010–2011 seasonal influenza vaccine. See MMWR 2010;59(No. 8):33–34.
8. **Measles, mumps, and rubella vaccine (MMR).** (Minimum age: 12 months)
 • The second dose may be administered before age 4 years, provided at least 4 weeks have elapsed since the first dose.
9. **Varicella vaccine.** (Minimum age: 12 months)
 • The second dose may be administered before age 4 years, provided at least 3 months have elapsed since the first dose.
 • For children aged 12 months through 12 years the recommended minimum interval between doses is 3 months. However, if the second dose was administered at least 4 weeks after the first dose, it can be accepted as valid.
10. **Hepatitis A vaccine (HepA).** (Minimum age: 12 months)
 • Administer 2 doses at least 6 months apart.
 • HepA is recommended for children aged older than 23 months who live in areas where vaccination programs target older children, who are at increased risk for infection, or for whom immunity against hepatitis A is desired.
11. **Meningococcal conjugate vaccine, quadrivalent (MCV4).** (Minimum age: 2 years)
 • Administer 2 doses of MCV4 at least 8 weeks apart to children aged 2 through 10 years with persistent complement component deficiency and anatomic or functional asplenia, and 1 dose every 5 years thereafter.
 • Persons with human immunodeficiency virus (HIV) infection who are vaccinated with MCV4 should receive 2 doses at least 8 weeks apart.
 • Administer 1 dose of MCV4 to children aged 2 through 10 years who travel to countries with highly endemic or epidemic disease and during outbreaks caused by a vaccine serogroup.
 • Administer MCV4 to children at continued risk for meningococcal disease who were previously vaccinated with MCV4 or meningococcal polysaccharide vaccine after 3 years if the first dose was administered at age 2 through 6 years.

The Recommended Immunization Schedules for Persons Aged 0 Through 18 Years are approved by the Advisory Committee on Immunization Practices (http://www.cdc.gov/vaccines/recs/acip), the American Academy of Pediatrics (http://www.aap.org), and the American Academy of Family Physicians (http://www.aafp.org).
Department of Health and Human Services • Centers for Disease Control and Prevention

Index